SKATING

FOR CROSS-COUNTRY SKIERS

**Audun Endestad
and John Teaford**

Leisure Press
Champaign, Illinois

Library of Congress Cataloging-in-Publication Data

Endestad, Audun, 1953-
  Skating for cross-country skiers.

  Includes index.
  1. Cross-country skiing—Training. 2. Skating.
  I. Teaford, John, 1961-   . II. Title.
  GV855.5.T73E53 1987   796.93   86-21298
  ISBN 0-88011-282-4

Developmental Editor: Vic MacKenzie
Copy Editor: Kevin Neely
Production Director: Ernie Noa
Typesetters: Sandra Meier and Brad Colson
Text Layout: Denise Mueller
Cover Photo: Lori Adamski-Peek
Back Cover Photos:
  Audun Endestad by Lori Adamski-Peek
  and John Teaford by Nancy Battaglia
Photographs: Pages 36 and 38 © Michael Kevin Daly;
  all other interior photographs © by Nancy Battaglia
Printed by: United Graphics

Front Cover: Audun Endestad competing for the
  USA ski team

ISBN: 0-88011-282-4

Printed in the United States of America

10 9 8 7 6 5 4 3 2 1

Leisure Press
A division of Human Kinetics Publishers, Inc.
Box 5076, Champaign, IL 61820

Contents

About
the Authors

Audun Endestad first became well known in the United States in February of 1984 when he won his battle for U.S. citizenship. That last-minute decision allowed him to represent this country in the Olympic Winter Games in Sarajevo, Yugoslavia. A native of Norway, Audun is currently the top-ranked American on both the World Cup and World Loppet circuits. He is a seven-time winner of the Australian National Championships, three-time overall marathon champion of the U.S. Ski Chase, and eight-time gold medalist at the U.S. National Championships. At present he is preparing for the upcoming race season with a long-range objective of representing the United States once again at the 1988 Olympic Winter Games in Calgary, Canada. He now resides in Fairbanks, Alaska.

John Teaford is an internationally competitive speed skater, avid Nordic skier, and mountaineer with expedition experience on four continents. He has worked at the Olympic Training Center in Marquette, Michigan and the Colorado Outward Bound School. He developed his ski technique theories while employed as a teacher at The Mountain House School, a secondary ski academy in Lake Placid, New York. He is a free-lance writer and is training for the upcoming speed skating season and the 1988 Olympic Trials. John spends a part of each skating season living in Inzell, West Germany and resides the remainder of the year in Madison, Wisconsin.

Preface

This is not a book on cross-country skiing. Any quality book on cross-country skiing would say something to skiers at all levels, from beginner to expert. It would cover all aspects of skiing and ski training and would guide skiers through all facets of the sport from beginning to end. This book does not pretend to be so complete. It covers all the aspects of skating on cross-country skis but does not include much of the general skiing information that has been covered in other fine books. *Caldwell on Cross-Country* by John Caldwell and *Ski Faster, Easier* by Lee Borowski both offer complete coverage on all other aspects of skiing. I consider this book to be merely a supplement to books of that type.

Skating for Cross-Country Skiers was written in response to a need in the skiing community. It is designed to serve the needs of the intermediate to advanced skier who is interested in understanding and using the new skating techniques. The only reason this book is necessary is that many differences exist in training and technique between cross-country skating and conventional skiing, and many skiers are training in the same way they always have when the demands of skating require a new type of training. A complete work on skating is needed, and I hope that this book will meet that need.

Much of the useful technical information on skating has not filtered down from the elite ranks, and many skiers have been forced to develop their own systems and ideas. Unfortunately, without a proper understanding of the basics of a skating stroke, many writers and coaches have been inadvertently misleading skiers with incorrect or incomplete instruction. The European skiing powers are practicing training techniques very similar to those used by speed skaters, but American skiers have been slow to pick up on these ideas. In *Skating for Cross-Country Skiers*, Audun and I have collaborated to combine the technique and training principles of speed skating and skiing in an attempt to offer the serious skier an overview of this exciting new technique.

We have attempted to cover all the aspects of skating that differ from conventional skiing. Any aspects of the sport that involve the same principles as conventional skiing, such as injuries, travel and training, general racing strategy, and ski preparation, we have left to other books that have already covered those topics in depth. *Skating for Cross-Country Skiers* covers complete skating mechanics and technique, as well as specific aspects of dryland and on-snow training. Chapters are included on weight training, equipment selection, imitation exercises, and the most specific forms of training, including training with roller skis, roller skates, and a slideboard. Numerous graphs and diagrams explain the actual workouts.

This book is designed to express one particular set of ideas. We do not intend to cater to every idea in the sport. We have some very set ideas about how skating should be taught, trained for, and performed. If some of these ideas are unpopular, the controversy can only help the sport. Skiing is not only changing, it already has changed. Our intention in this book is to keep you abreast of the most recent changes. Open-mindedness will be very important in the skiing world in the years to come. We hope that the information in this book will give you a base for interpreting the innovations that are yet to come in cross-country skiing.

John Teaford

Acknowledgments

This book began as such a simple project, almost as a whim. I am constantly surprised at how much work it has required, and how many people have been involved. First I must acknowledge the help received from Vic MacKenzie of Human Kinetics Publishers, who served as the book's developmental editor. His gentle prodding and constant attention to detail are responsible for the quality of presentation in this book. It would not have been possible without Vic's guidance and encouragement.

I must also mention the knowledge I gained from Bob Corby, former coach of the U.S. National Speed Skating Team, in the years I spent training under him and following his training programs. I attribute much of the information in this book to the many hours he spent patiently answering my many questions. I must also thank Andrew Barron for his critical reviews of the early drafts of this book and the technical information he provided to us.

I began this project while living and working in Lake Placid, New York. I must thank the people of that community for making me feel welcome and accepting me as a harmless immigrant. I am particularly indebted to Gail Meyer for her ace typing skills and to Ed Finnerty, legal counsel extraordinaire. My luckiest find in Lake Placid was Nancy Battaglia, whose patience, perseverance, and talent are responsible for the magnificent photographs in the following pages.

A special thanks goes out to Peter VanWyk whose constant companionship and twisted sense of humor allowed me to maintain some semblance of sanity through the tough early stages of this project.

John Teaford

Introduction

By now most of you have heard the story of how Bill Koch was passed by an unknown skier during a European marathon race and how he stepped in behind to copy this faster skier's technique. Bill eventually went on to use this "skating" technique to become the first non-European to capture the Nordic World Cup and forever change the technical nature of competitive cross-country skiing. Since that time skiers have been experimenting with the techniques of skating on cross-country skis as a full-time technique.

By the time of the World Championships in Seefeld, Austria, in 1985, skating had been universally accepted by competitors in the international cross-country scene. All medals at that competition were won by skiers who used glide wax only and skated the entire course. Skiers all over the world and at all levels of competition have begun skating exclusively when it is allowed. There can be no argument that, under certain conditions, skating is significantly faster than conventional skiing, and competitive skiers have been quick to pursue the new techniques.

Because of the recent competitive results, some people in the international skiing community feared that skating might replace conventional kick-and-glide techniques altogether. There was also talk of outlawing skating in racing events. Either of these situations would have been harmful to the sport of skiing. Racers will always be interested in going as fast as possible, but many recreational skiers are not interested in learning skating techniques. Skating techniques are not very efficient at the comfortable speeds most recreational skiers use, and recreational skiers do not appreciate having the tracks obliterated by skating skiers. Skiers are interested in preserving the athletic beauty of conventional skiing, and in 1986 concessions were made to tradition. The 1986 Nordic World Cup and World Master's Championships were divided into conventional and freestyle (skating allowed) events. Many local skiing events are being arranged in similar formats to allow skiers to compete in races where they are comfortable with the technique. It looks as though skating has been accepted as a legitimate technique and is here to stay.

This book is not intended to advocate replacing conventional skiing with skating techniques. Skating is not the best technique for many skiers. Beginners, tourers, and noncompetitive skiers often feel perfectly comfortable with conventional techniques and the more natural feel of kick and glide. Young children take very readily to the techniques of skating, but it would be a pity to grow up without being able to perform all the styles of cross-country skiing. The new split schedule used in many competitions will guarantee that all skiing techniques, new and old, will be preserved, and this is as it should be.

This book has been written to address the differences between the techniques and training principles of conventional skiing versus skating on cross-country skis. Training and techniques for skating on cross-country skis are now closer to speed skating than to conventional skiing. That's why Audun and I decided to collaborate in an effort to combine the principles of speed skating and cross-country skiing. This is a new approach to skiing, and we hope it will be well received.

Many skiers may have difficulty accepting the instructions and principles of a speed skater. But much of the skating instruction skiers have received through the media has been the result of hopeful innovations made by skiers and ski coaches who do not thoroughly understand the goals and directions of training for skating or the basic technical elements of a skating stroke. Skiers began pursuing skating at a competitive level before they completely understood the most basic principles of performing a skating stroke. Much of the technical information dispersed in the last few years has not addressed these considerations. Instead, most technical information has been directed at fine points such as tempo and body position without considering how a skating stroke actually works. This book attempts to look at cross-country skating as a total sport, from its most basic elements to the small technical refinements sought by the racer.

Speed skaters have spent years pursuing a technique that is identical to that used on cross-country skis and searching for the best way to augment that technique with dryland training. Perhaps the only factor that has kept skiers from pursuing the knowledge held by speed skaters has been the idea that speed skating and cross-country skating are somehow different technically. The better skiers become at skating, however, the more they realize the direct technical relationships that exist between speed skating and cross-country skating. *Skating for Cross-Country Skiers* is the first attempt to combine the techniques of these two sports in a work that is designed to address all the questions and technical problems experienced by the intermediate to advanced skier.

Figure 1.1 Igor Shulekin of the Soviet Union displays good skating technique during the 1986 World Junior Championships. Cross-country skating has replaced conventional skiing techniques in freestyle races from local league competitions to the World Cup.

Basic
Mechanics
of the
Skating Stroke

A number of different stroke types, stroke tempos, and individual styles for skating on cross-country skis will be presented later in the book. Before we can discuss the finer points of skating for cross-country skiers, however, we need to establish the basics we can all agree upon and refer back to so that explaining the technical intricacies in later chapters will be easier and more understandable (see Figure 1.1).

This chapter does not deal with skiing specifically. Rather it describes the elements involved in any lateral skating stroke. What we will be describing are the elements involved in gaining momentum from a lateral push, as well as the small technical elements that comprise each stroke. If the next few pages don't sound like skiing to you, that's because the mechanical skills we are describing happen so quickly that most observers don't see them at all. The purpose of this chapter is to give the reader a feel for the basic rules of skating (see Figure 1.2).

Basic Stroke Mechanics

We have broken down the basic skating stroke into five parts that, when performed with fluidity and

Figure 1.2 Although skating has captured the spotlight on the competitive scene, any complete skier will still have command of all cross-country skiing techniques. Here Audun displays excellent diagonal technique during the 1984 Olympic Trials.

grace, will help you to glide across the snow with significantly increased speed. This is not, however, a chapter on how to skate. It is a chapter directed at increasing your understanding of the stroke and explaining, or discrediting, some of the current notions about skating on skis.

Figure 1.3 1. Load-up. 2. Primary weight transfer. Notice the shift of
the hips. 3-4. Push and secondary weight transfer. Still leading with
the hip, feet parallel to direction of travel, both heels in contact with
the ground, body pointed straight down the track. 5. Standing
recovery phase.

The basic skating stroke consists of the following five sequential parts:

1. Load-up
2. Primary weight transfer
3. Heel push
4. Secondary weight transfer and heel snap
5. Recovery

These are the primary technical phases involved in every skating stroke, whether on ice skates, roller skis, or cross-country skis, uphill, downhill, or on the flat. Let's take a closer look at each one (see Figure 1.3).

1. Load-Up

Load-up is the term we use to describe the initial phase of the stroke. You can't push if your knees aren't bent, and this initial bending of the knees is what presses your weight into the snow. The load-up is that process of bending your knees and "loading up" the weight on your pushing ski. It sounds simple enough, but very few skiers do it correctly, and many don't load up at all.

If you stand still on a wooden floor with squeaky floorboards with your knees straight, the boards won't make any noise. If, however, you suddenly bend your knees and let your weight drop, you will hear a complaining creak from the boards, indicating that you have magically increased your weight on the floor. (This exercise also works nicely on a bathroom scale.) This is the effect we are trying to achieve in the load-up phase: putting some extra pounds into the snow to begin a strong push that will be long and powerful, without slipping.

To get a feeling for how the load-up phase of the stroke works, position yourself with your left hand on a wall or pole and stand straight legged on your right foot. Keep that foot pointed straight ahead and concentrate your weight on the middle to rear half of the foot. All that is required to increase your weight on the floor (or snow) is to make those imaginary floorboards creak. Bend your standing knee quickly (using the wall for balance), drop your weight straight down, and place your left foot down lightly on the floor beside and slightly ahead of your right foot.

This is the end of the load-up. The deeper and more quickly you drop the knees, the more weight and power you will be transmitting down onto the snow.

In most strokes, this would also be the point at which you would plant the poles. If you did this same exercise with poles in your hands, the tips should have touched the ground as soon as you began bending your knees. Accomplished skaters will plant their poles, rather delicately, with this bend of the knees, not drive them down into the snow with the arms and shoulders as in the traditional "double pole." The poling motion that will be used in conjunction with all skating strokes is both quicker and more subtle than the old double-poling motion, but we'll deal with poling in greater detail later in the book.

If you do try this drill with poles in your hands, you will immediately discover that with your knees deeply bent, your hands are trapped atop your poles and high above your head, like a baby being walked by a proud parent. Realize that you will never be in this position on the snow. By the time you would have completed loading up the stroke and reached your lowest position before the pushing phase actually be-gan, your poles would have been planted and would al-ready have passed by your hips, instead of leaving you looking the victim of a holdup.

2. Primary Weight Transfer

Primary weight transfer is not that crucial weight transfer that all those coaches and articles have been warning you about. That one will come soon enough. Primary weight transfer is the one the coaches and articles have been neglecting.

The primary weight transfer is a very small, almost imperceptible motion that is every bit as crucial as the four other phases of any skating stroke. It is the basis of all the power in your stroke, and it is begun with a slight weight shift of the hips, like a hula dancer in slow motion. This is the start of lateral mo-tion in the stroke and begins as a hula shift of the hips

away from the pushing foot. Exaggerate it when you
practice it.

The weight of your upper body should still stay
over the pushing foot. All you have done is to shift
your weight to the inside of the pushing foot, without
shifting your weight off of the rear half of the foot. In
other words, keep your weight on your heels. You do
not need to consciously think of rolling the pushing ski
over onto the inside edge; this will happen naturally in
any technically correct stroke.

This is the point where the "push" in the stroke
actually begins, but realize that a skating stroke is not
really "lateral." The push is directed *down* onto the
snow, not out across it. At the end of this "hula transfer," your weight should be passing straight down into
the snow through the inside edge of your ski. This
pressure is what will keep your push from slipping,
not the actual angle at which the ski is tilted over onto
its edge.

Now try the two steps in conjunction, standing
there next to the wall: the load-up followed by that
subtle but ever so intoxicating hula.

3. Heel Push

Now we will get down to the real "push and
shove" of skating. Move back over to the wall and go
through the load-up and hula phases again, remembering to keep your weight on your pushing heel.

At this point, begin straightening the pushing leg
while keeping your weight on the rear half of the foot.
You will need to place your free (left) foot about 20-30
centimeters from the wall in order to accept the transfer of weight that will come in the next step. In placing
the free foot, make sure that you are stepping directly
toward the wall. Directing the stroke to the side is
vital, and we'll spend much of the remainder of this
book explaining why. Most skiers are in the habit of
doing this drill by stepping forward and to the left, rolling the push off of the toe. This is a bad habit, probably an imbedded remnant of the diagonal stride that
they practiced for so long. It is a habit to rid yourself
of now. The push should be generated from the rear
half of the foot and directed straight to the side.

This is the midpoint of the stroke, but by this time most of the power you will generate has already gone into the snow. Any gargantuan effort applied after this point is wasted and will only throw you off balance. Instead, what happens is called a *heel snap,* and it will be covered in the next phase of the stroke.

So now you are standing next to the wall with your knees bent, with most of your weight still on the right (pushing) foot, and leaning heavily against your left hand on the wall. Your left (free) foot should be delicately placed parallel to the wall and ready to absorb Step 4, the secondary weight transfer.

4. Secondary Weight Transfer and Heel Snap

From the midpush position (at the end of Step 3, above) all you need to do to accomplish this weight transfer is put that free (left) foot firmly down on the floor and continue straightening the right leg until all weight rests on the left leg, which is still deeply bent (90-110 degrees). As you complete the push, give your right knee a slight snap to the straightened position, and in doing so lift the toes of the right foot a bit off the floor. This "toes-up" finish position will indicate that your push did take place off the rear of the foot and that every ounce of power found its way into the snow, not into postrace excuses. The toes-up finish will be a common part of all lateral exercises described later in the book.

5. Recovery

If you have followed the first four steps correctly, then the recovery is a cinch. Just stand up. As you do stand up on that left leg, your right leg (which has become the free leg for the next push) will naturally follow your hips into position and will fall alongside the left foot to prepare for a new stroke.

As you stand up, your free foot should fall into place slightly ahead of the weight-bearing foot. This is called a *standing recovery position* and will be seen as the end of a marathon skating stroke. Recently, skiers have begun using skating styles more like that of speed skaters, in which the recovery of balance occurs without "standing." This *low recovery* will be covered in the discussion of stroke types in chapter 4. Either way, after the recovery, the push is completed and you are prepared to begin another stroke.

A Little Technique. The primary variable in the skating motion (and what might be making the local hotshot better than you) is how deep you choose to sit (in terms of degree of knee bend) for each stroke. For the power of each push to last longer (which is obviously desirable), the skier must assume a deeper knee bend and lower body position in general. This will require more strength and coordination. We intend to spend the remainder of this book telling you why this is important and suggesting ways to get these qualities into your skiing (see Figure 1.4).

Now that you know how to walk through the basic lower body stroke, we'll begin getting into detail, piecing together all the phases of the skating stroke.

Figure 1.4 Cross-country skating techniques can add a new dimension to the repertoire of skiers at almost any level of expertise.

Skating Checklist

The unfair thing about all these new skating techniques—and the real reason behind most of the protests against them, official and unofficial—is that this new method of propulsion has completely reshuffled the competitive deck at all levels of skiing, from local citizen's races to the world championships. Many of you are accomplished skiers who are comfortable with your technique and the training requirements of traditional skiing. This was fine until some innovative skiers all but changed the rules and made much of what you knew or expected in skiing obsolete.

We don't believe that we need to apologize for innovation. We do, however, feel that there is a need to clear up the conflicting information that makes skating proficiency unreachable for many eager skiers. Let's start with the facts on why it's worth your while to master the techniques of skating on skis. You know that skaters are winning races; here's how they are doing it.

Is Skating Actually Faster?

Using a diagonal stride or conventional double-pole, skiers can propel themselves forward only as fast as they can push back. Cross-country skaters, on the other hand, can sustain pressure for a much longer period of time on the snow and, by using lateral force against a gliding ski that cannot move sideways, they can propel themselves forward along the track. This is the same principle that dictates that a canoe can only move forward as fast as the campers can paddle it, paddling straight back as you would push in a diagonal stride. A sailboat, however, by planting its keel in the water (like a ski "tracking") to prevent it from slipping sideways, can convert a "lateral" wind of 20 kilometers per hour into a forward propulsion (ideally) of 20-25 kilometers per hour.

This is as technical as we feel we need to get. The *maximum* flat rates of travel are as follows:

- diagonal stride = 5-7 meters/second
- double-poling = 7-8 meters/second
- skating = 10-11 meters/second

Combine this information with the facts that proficient skaters no longer need kick wax on their skis (and can thus avoid the added drag) and that a skating stride has no built-in stopping point (unlike in a diagonal stride, where one must "set the wax" every stroke). The result is that under most conditions, skating is going to be significantly faster than conventional styles of skiing.

Skating does have disadvantages, however. It is very inefficient at low speeds, especially on uphills, which means that the physical price you pay in climbing a hill is very high when compared to whatever advantage might be gained from skating. Nevertheless, the overall advantage, the increase in mean speed, is more than enough to convince most skiers that it's worth their while to learn to master these techniques.

Now that you know that learning the skating stroke is important and have resolved yourself to the task of learning it properly, here are the ten keys to success in the slippery world of cross-country skating:

Skating Checklist

1. Sit back
2. Load up
3. Lead with the hips
4. Maintain quiet upper body
5. Maintain proper body position/posture
6. Maintain heel contact

7. Concentrate on correct direction of push
8. Shorten the poling motion
9. Maintain adequate knee bend
10. Relax and enjoy yourself

These are the things to look for and concentrate on during every skating stroke. Now let's look at each one in detail.

1. Sit Back

It's a wise person who learns the most important element first, and in cross-country skating sitting back is it. If you don't learn to "sit back" and keep your weight on the middle of your foot, none of the instructions in this book will work.

Sitting back does not mean *leaning back*. Sitting back simply means that the push will be generated from the middle of the foot (as opposed to the toes) and that you should always try your best to keep your feet in front of, or at least even with, your hips. Allowing your feet to fall behind the hips will cause you to generate the push from the toes.

The power skiers can generate is a direct result of their weight acting against the snow. If a loaded ski can't skid sideways, it must go some other direction to release all the force you have put onto it. If you sit back, the ski will travel forward. On the other hand, if you let your weight fall forward onto the ball of the foot, the ski will travel backwards, with no kick wax to give it purchase.

Here's something you can do to test the sit-back theory in the privacy of your own home.

Testing the Sit-Back Theory.   Take a roller ski out of the closet (one with ratcheted wheels will work best) and find a bare floor or firm carpet and a few feet of open wall space to lean against. Stand with your right foot on the ski as though you were wearing a ski boot and had it in the binding. Reach out with the left hand to touch the wall for balance.

Standing on that ski, bend your right knee deeply (90-105 degrees), but intentionally keep your weight on the *toes*. When you get down there, let your left arm bend, leaning your weight against the wall. Now, *slowly* shift your weight from toes to heel, and *hang on* because that ski is going to scoot forward.

Magic has taken over, and you have created forward motion without ever pushing back but by simply utilizing pressure and weight shift on a loaded ski. This is the way skating should be made to work on cross-country skis. Skating will always function as a result of forcing the pushing ski to glide *forward*, never by "scooter pushing" against the edge of the ski (like on a skateboard). The downward pressure of the ski is what gives you traction, not the fact that the ski is rolled over onto its edge. Even an edged ski will slip if not enough weight is applied to it.

Even most world-class skiers don't sit back fully and are constantly directing their push slightly to the rear and pushing off the toe. Obviously, their level of fitness is largely responsible for their level of success, but bad technique will not win many races. Just look at the advantage you've gained over the competition by knowing to sit back while you ski, and we are only at the beginning of the list!

Patience.   The other vital advantage that sitting back will provide for you is to keep you patient. Skating is an exhausting mode of propulsion that uses large muscle groups and requires long periods of static muscle activity. The idea is not to constantly increase your speed, but rather to constantly *maintain* it. If you decide to chase that rascal ahead of you in the tracks, most likely you will get out ahead of your skis (leaning forward, getting up on the toes, and inadvertently pushing back), trying too hard, too fast. Doing this will spoil the efficiency of your stroke when you need it most, and that rascal will continue to stay ahead of you while you struggle even harder.

It's better to think of accelerating more in terms of slowly "tightening the screws": sitting a little deeper, picking up the tempo slightly, and concentrating on increasing the pressure on the snow. Patience is the key. Too much energy can be wasted in the skating motion. When you want to accelerate, do it over the next 30 strokes, not in the next three.

The line between maintaining speed and physically hitting the wall is finer in skating than in conventional skiing, and the physical price is higher for whatever tactical or technical mistakes you make. Make a few too many mistakes and you might as well stop at the next aid station on the course and volunteer to help pass out Gatorade and orange slices!

2. Load Up

You must go straight down and "load up" the pressure of the pushing ski before the skating stroke can begin. That means that every stroke can be thought to have two parts: one vertical and the second lateral. An observer would not normally discern a separation between these two halves of the stroke because it happens very quickly. With every stroke, you must build the pressure before the pushing can commence.

As a skier, you know how devastating a slip can be, especially on an uphill. So load up that pushing foot and make it too heavy to slip. If you can load up each stroke and keep your weight on the backs of your boots, then you are already a fast skier.

3. Lead With the Hips

Okay, you are sitting back and you are loading up, but still something is missing. In a case like this, where you are doing everything right and still getting mediocre results, it is best to look for that almost invisible variable that better skiers may be performing better than you. Let's take a look at hip orientation.

In skiing, as in all sports, your hips must always be in line with your shoulders and the rest of your body, and in the case of skating your hips must be constantly *perpendicular* to the line of travel. Think of skiing with a pencil in your navel and constantly pointing it straight down the track.

A good technical skier initiates the push with the hips. The "hula shift" is where the push begins, and thus the hips will lead the rest of the body through the push. A front view of a skier at the highest force point of the push should show that the free hip is leading the entire body into the push. Never will the leading be done by the upper body (shoulders). That way you can avoid twisting and keep your pushes going in the right direction.

Until the final weight transfer, your sternum (mid-chest) should remain over the big toe of the pushing foot. This will feel very awkward at first, but it is the best way to keep your body weight over the pushing foot for the longest possible time and thereby get the most out of each push. Letting the upper body stay over the push means that you must lead with the free hip. Anyone who leads with the shoulders is actually taking weight—and therefore power—away from each push.

Prove It to Yourself. Let's do another trick to prove this point to the skeptical. You already know that the power in your push is going to travel through the heel and that whenever you raise the pushing heel you are actually "deloading" the push. With that fact in mind, let's try a little experiment.

Find a sheet of paper and fold it down the middle. Stand up straight, and have a friend place the folded edge of the paper under the toes of your right foot so that it touches the sole of your shoe but the fold is not flattened out by your toes. Now all you have to do is begin a normal load-up. Your weight will stay on the rear half of your foot. When you get about halfway down, turn your upper body to the left as though you were about to start a push and watch your toes flatten out the folded paper. This is the way most of us ski all the time. Before the stroke could even happen, we shifted the weight to the toes (flattening out the paper), and the push was directed back instead of directly to the side. This technique results in less weight, less power, less speed.

Now, let's try the same trick again. But this time, instead of turning the upper body in the middle of the load-up, keep your chest centered over the pushing foot (the one on the paper). Your weight should rest naturally on the rear of the pushing foot. When you go to push, leaving the upper body over the pushing foot and forcing yourself to lead with the free hip (moving to the left), the fold in the paper should remain unchanged. When you can push without flattening out the paper, you have mastered the skating stroke.

Remember that none of these demonstrations will work unless you concentrate on pushing straight out to the side.

4. Maintain Quiet Upper Body

By "upper body," we are referring to above the waist and by "quiet" we mean almost no unnecessary movement of any kind. Of course, you have to use your poles, but you can pole without thrashing your head and shoulders about or leading with your upper body. Movement in the upper body not only causes you to pull your weight away from the pushing foot, causing you to slip, but it also requires a very high energy expenditure to maintain all that extra movement.

Many people make the mistake of equating increased energy output with increased speed. Nothing could be further from the truth. Just tell someone to go faster or to try to hang on when they are struggling and watch their performance fall apart technically. Let the upper body stay over the push. Don't put on a show with lots of wasted movement. Let your chest and shoulders just go along for the ride, while you are sitting back and pointing your pencil down the track (see Figure 2.1).

5. Maintain Proper Body Posture

Illusions are a big part of the confusion in sports, and body posture is a good example. If you ask anyone what speed skaters look like, they'll tell you they are all bent over. But that is not necessarily true. If skaters or skiers were to bend over from the hips, their body weight would be concentrated on the toes. Correct technique emphasizes generating the push from the midfoot, and skaters and skiers are capable of this type of push, even though they use a lower body position.

Speed skaters use what is called a *cat-back*. Skiers would do well to develop a similar body posture. Skaters are able to keep their shoulders low and

Figure 2.1 Kari Swenson of the U.S. Biathlon Team shows good skating technique on the flat as she leaves the shooting area. She is in a hurry to get back up to speed, yet her stroke is not rushed and her upper body remains relaxed.

rounded (i.e., relaxed) by letting their spines curve down while still keeping their weight on the heels and sitting back, thus creating the "bent over" illusion. They are not bending at the hips. The push in skiing is generally shorter than in speed skating so that skiers do not absolutely need the extreme body position that speed skaters use, but a relaxed and low body position will help to increase the length and efficiency of each stroke.

"The Miracle That Made a Man Out of Mack." Do you remember the old Charles Atlas ads in the backs of the comic books? The ones where the bully kicks sand in the wimp's face? The cartoon was entitled "The Miracle That Made a Man Out of Mack." You can use this cartoon and its illustrations as a reminder of the type of body posture we are recommending for skating skiers.

We know that your upper body must be strong enough to keep up with the demands of poling, but your posture should resemble Mack's before the "miracle." Let your chest disappear and your shoulders fall and slouch in a totally relaxed manner, as though you had just let out a great sigh. You must keep a vision of your upper body as small, compact, and relaxed. Remember that the poling motion you will be using will be smaller, quicker, and more subtle than a normal double-pole. Any wasted effort, especially unnecessary thrashing of the head, shoulders, and arms, can have a disastrous effect on your ability to maintain smooth technique.

Try to keep your elbows close to your sides and use as little unnecessary movement in the upper body as possible. As you ski, you will be a 98-pound weakling, a sunken-chested wimp, with your power and technique hidden from view behind a quiet, efficient body posture. Stay calm under stress, don't waste energy that you can't afford to lose, and let your competitors wonder how you went so fast with "so little effort." Visualize "Mack before the miracle."

6. Maintain Heel Contact

By now you should know that the push in skating is generated from the heel, but this is another opportunity to remind you of how extremely important this bit of instruction really is. We have continually received or overheard information from coaches at all levels of skiing, and from nationally respected magazines, that skiers should push with the toe. This is dead wrong and is responsible for about half of the major technical problems that we observe. The push in any type of skating motion—whether on ice, snow, on roller skis, roller skates, slideboards, or during dryland exercises—should come from the *heel.*

The argument over "toe push" or "heel push" is made even more difficult by still photography and the technical information that misinformed people take from the work of photographers who don't even ski themselves. In almost every skating photo, the photographer snapped the picture at the point of the skier's greatest extension. Why not? That's the prettiest picture. The problem for skiers who are studying such photos for the technical information they can provide is that the pictures are lying. The pointed toe at the end of the push is *not* a part of the force; it is a reaction to the amount of force generated.

The point at which the picture was taken was long after the actual pushing had concluded; the skier had already begun the recovery phase. In so doing he has relaxed the pushing leg and taken the weight off of the ski. When this is done, the tail of the ski drops, making it look as if the push was made with the toe. The net effect of this type of picture on the skiing public is that many people are now actively trying to push with the toe. Our only advice is don't do it. *Always* generate the push from the heel.

A toe push will involve body mechanics exactly opposite to those we have been trying to introduce. A skier pushing with the toe will sit forward, push back instead of directly to the side, lead with the shoulders, skip the load-up entirely, and slip a lot. A toe push will let you think you look like the stars in all the skiing ads in the magazines, but it will also destroy your skiing career. Don't be fooled by photographers.

The idea of pushing with the heel is probably too extreme for most of you to believe. What we are trying to say in making such a statement is that almost all of the power in a skating stroke comes from the first two thirds of the stroke, long before your pushing knee has straightened. If a skier persists in transferring the weight to the toes too soon in a push, then the time available to generate pressure and power will be shortened. After you get over the shock of the term *heel push*, you will come to realize what we mean is that a skier must maintain heel contact with the ski for as long as possible on each stroke. Doing this one little thing will force you to do everything else correctly: bending the knees, sitting back, and pushing as directly to the side as possible.

A heel push really does happen on roller skates or ice skates, partly because they are shorter and more maneuverable than skis (i.e., they allow the heel to "come around" with each push) and partly because both roller and ice skates are faster than skis, giving each stroke better runout. By exaggerating this heel push technique, you accustom your body to performing the motions of the best skating stroke. In this way you will constantly prepare yourself to strive for the optimum technique with each push. This is the key to skating success. Holding optimum technique as much as possible with each stroke and practicing heel contact is the best start possible.

7. Concentrate on Correct Direction of Push

A heel push allows correct direction of push, and pushing directly out to the side requires your weight to be concentrated on the heel. These two steps on the checklist are inseparable.

By directing the push out to the side (as opposed to trying to push slightly back), you can increase the length of time your loaded stroke will be transferring weight onto the snow. Keep in mind that the force of the push is still being directed *down* onto the snow and that the release of this force is what makes the ski travel. What we are suggesting in this section is that the skier should attempt to guide the ski directly to the side, as much as possible, in releasing the force of the push.

Many situations are not ideal for skating, such as any time you are moving at a slow rate of speed. On uphills, for example, you will need to alter your technique to keep from getting slowed to a walk. Even in these situations it is still best to keep trying to push as much as possible directly to the side. The two things that will change are the stroke tempo and the angle of the pushing ski in relation to the gliding ski. The lower the speed you are able to maintain (whether due to an uphill, slow snow, fatigue, or bad weather

conditions) the quicker the stroke tempo (i.e., the number of strokes per minute) should be and the wider the
angle will become between the pushing and gliding
skis. "Wider ski angle" does not mean "pushing back."

Your mission in these situations is to stay as close
as possible to ideal form, and that means pushing
directly to the side. Keep sitting back and keep your
feet in front of your hips. As soon as your pushing foot
drops behind your hips, the heel will come off the ski,
the ski will stop gliding (because you have weighted
the tip), and you will be "scooter pushing" up the hill.
This is not a pretty sight.

Later we will present an entire section on stroke
mechanics for specific conditions or terrain on a course
and when and how to best use each stroke type. For
now, suffice to say that your push should always be
directed as much as possible to the side, with pushing
skis remaining as parallel as possible to the line of
travel. This implies that the pushing ski will be traveling forward at approximately the same rate of speed as
the gliding ski. It won't ever stop or slow down to
push. Slowing the ski to push is a bad habit that many
people acquire in the summer on roller skis or skates.
Get it out of your head now. Don't be wasting time
when you could be skiing fast.

8. Shorten the Poling Motion

The poling motion you will want to utilize in conjunction with skating will be much more abbreviated
than a traditional double-pole. It will still be powerful,
but quicker and without a full "bow" of the upper
body used in the double-pole. To begin with, you
should no longer begin the double-pole in the totally
upright position used in the more classical styles, nor
will you want to get out over your toes. You may end
up feeling slightly rushed to get your poling in on
time, especially with the longer poles used with skating. As you get accustomed to the feel of skating, however, you will feel how nicely the skate and the
double-pole or diagonal-pole (and their variations) go
together.

As you remember from descriptions of the load-up,
the poles are usually planted as a result of the initial

knee bend. After planting, the job for your arms is to get the poles past your hips and out of the way as fast as possible without losing too much power in the process. This is done by the use of a shorter, quicker stroke, in which your elbows will always stay very close to your body. The entire motion will stop soon after your hands have passed your hips.

With a lateral stroke like skating in which a quick stroke tempo is one of the keys to success, you no longer have time for a long, extended poling motion. We are not saying this new motion should be so short that it is ineffective, only that the power should be placed more accurately and explosively. You should think of your hands as passing close by your ribs, as opposed to going down past the knees as in the conventional double-pole. You must get those poles out the back and be ready to recover as early as possible.

9. Maintain Adequate Knee Bend

You can't begin to accomplish any of the techniques described so far unless you bend your knees. And we mean *bend your knees.* The deeper the knee bend the more weight you can load onto the ski and the longer you can make the stroke. That all adds up to increased speed.

Here's the catch. Skating with a low knee bend is (a) hard on the knees, (b) highly inefficient in terms of energy conservation, and (c) still absolutely necessary, even after considering its drawbacks. Sitting low and staying in control without completely exploding from lactic acid overdose must become one of the primary elements in determining how you train, both on snow and during the dryland season.

Staying deep with a low knee bend requires three things: great leg strength (primarily in the gluteals, hamstrings, and quadriceps, in that order of importance); delicate balance (to allow you to sit deep without rocking forward onto your toes); and the ability to continually wash your system free of lactic acid, an ability that is gained from specific physical training. These are the goals of a specific skating training program, which will be described in chapters 5 through 10.

Knee Bend and Distance.   The shorter the race, the more power you can afford to put into each stroke. Therefore, the shorter the distance to be skied at speed, the deeper the knee bend you should attempt to maintain. Conversely, the longer the distance, the higher your sitting position should be to conserve energy and to keep your effort aerobic.

10. Relax and Enjoy Yourself

By now you are probably wondering "How do I remember all this?" Well, the key to further success is to enjoy skating.

Every time you ski, remember the basics that we have already covered. Pick one detail every day on which to concentrate. In this way you can break down your own knowledge of skating and get your training partners to help point out each other's strengths and weaknesses. When you don't think you can stand it any longer, put on some kick wax and go remind your-self that skiing is your sport. You are a good skier and on the way to becoming even better. You won't always be a beginner, and it won't always feel awkward. Try to relax and enjoy it.

Specific Styles 3

Strokes, Tempo, Terrain, Conditions

Now that you have a working knowledge of the skating stroke, we can begin putting all the information together into a workable system. In this chapter we'll explore exactly how to perform the numerous stroke variations and show you when and how to use each to its best advantage.

A skiing course is not a speed skating oval, where one type of stroke is best to perform at all times. Compared to speed skating in skiing the speeds are so low, the courses and conditions so variable, and the distances so great that it is to your advantage to learn a number of different stroke types and poling patterns for use in different situations, such as on particular parts of the course, during bad conditions, or when a certain body part needs rest.

In other words, no single skating stroke is best for skiers, unlike for speed skaters, so you need to learn them all. Let's begin breaking down the various skating strokes by giving them names. In these brief descriptions, we mention variations and the primary usage of each stroke. The stroke types are not explained here but are fully described later in this chapter (see Figure 3.1).

Symmetrical v-skate (SVS) involves alternating pushing skis with each stroke, combined with either a diagonal poling motion (using one arm at a time, also called *single-stick*), or a double-poling motion on each stroke (sometimes called *double-stick*). SVS employs a low recovery phase (i.e., straightening the legs only in the stroke itself, never in the recovery). It is best used on slow- to medium-speed uphills or in accelerating from a standing start. SVS is used at low or medium speeds with a high stroke tempo and has three varia-

Figure 3.1 Speed skater in midstroke. Note that the entire blade is in contact with the ice and that the body is oriented down the track without any twisting. Stroke mechanics for skating and for skiers is identical. The only difference is in the lower body position.

tions including single-stick, double-stick, and without poles.

Marathon skate is pushing with only one ski (the gliding ski in the track), combining each push with a double-pole. It is best used on downhills and high-speed flats. It is a high-speed stroke, utilizing low stroke tempo and has four variations, including marathon, marathon tuck, inside marathon turn, and outside marathon turn.

Asymmetrical v-skate is a skating stroke alternating pushing skis with each stroke (both skis out of the tracks) but using a double-pole on only one side of the stroke and recovering the poles while the skating push takes place on the other side (i.e., there are half as many poling motions as skating strokes). It is best used on moderate uphills or on medium-speed flats with medium speed and medium to high stroke tempo. There are two variations, including AVS and AVS stagger-pole.

Herringbone is the same stroke used by conventional skiers. There are times on extremely steep uphills when running would be quicker than to try to keep gliding; that is when you'll use a herringbone. It is simply running on the inside edges of your skis, which are widely angled, coordinated with a single-stick poling motion. This stroke is used at the lowest speed, with the highest tempo and no glide.

These are what we have found to be the four basic divisions from which all current skating techniques are derived. By the time you read this, additional styles may be evolving. The techniques and strategies that will be described in this chapter make a fine repertoire for any skier and give you a knowledge of the basics complete enough to help you in deciding whether or not new innovations will be worthwhile.

Symmetrical V-Skate

SVS is the most versatile of the skating motions. It can be used in a variety of tempos and with either a double-pole or a diagonal poling motion. This versatility allows it to be used for initiating movement from a standstill or in gaining or maintaining speed on uphills and flats. It is also the most practical stroke for skating in extremely adverse conditions such as soft snow or bad track because it depends less on glide and more on push and stroke tempo than any other stroke type. Using a symmetrical v-skate, you are generating power to the snow more regularly and more consistently than with any other stroke. "Gliding" means slowing down. You do less gliding and more pushing with a symmetrical v-skate than in any other stroke.

In bad conditions and on uphills, it is to your advantage to rely more heavily on push than on glide so that the technique, which can be performed at a very high tempo and allows the highest ratio of push to glide, will yield the best results. SVS is that technique. Because of its symmetry (both sides of the stroke are equal), SVS is also probably the best method to teach beginners their first time out. Otherwise, beginners may automatically develop a strong side and a weak side (see Figure 3.2).

Figure 3.2 Excellent SVS technique on roller skates. Notice the low but relaxed body position. This shows the moment of greatest force of this particular stroke, and all four wheels of the pushing skate are still in contact with the ground.

Too Much Tempo? Tempo is not the only thing that matters in skiing. In the past year many skiers and coaches have been making too big a deal of it. In dealing with v-skate strokes (excluding the marathon) there comes a point where constantly increasing the tempo has negative returns on mean speed. Skiing is a gliding sport, and if stroke tempos continue to become faster and faster, depending more and more on push than on glide, then eventually skiers will be literally "running."

Don't get carried away by suggestions of what the real secret to skating might be. A good skier does everything well, and the best tempo for you is most likely the quickest one that you can maintain comfortably without losing your balance or inhibiting your glide.

Symmetrical V-Skate Variations. SVS has three basic variations.

Double-Stick. The double-stick variation involves medium to fast tempo at medium to fast rate of speed.

It is used with a double-pole in conjunction with each skating stroke.

Single-Stick. Single-stick employs a fast tempo at the lowest rate of speed (from a standing start or on an extreme uphill where your speed is about to die) with a diagonal poling motion (i.e., a single-pole with each alternating stroke). A herringbone is simply a single-stick SVS with no glide. When the going gets even too slow for single-stick, it's time to resort to the herringbone.

Without Poles. At highest speeds, SVS can be used effectively as exactly the same stroke one would see on a speed skating track. The arms will swing alternately, without planting the poles, simply swinging for rhythm and momentum. In using this technique, arm swing becomes important for maintaining momentum, but it can also throw you off drastically. The no-poles technique involves swinging the arms straight forward and back, never crossing the center line of the body. This will help you to keep from twisting. Balance is very tricky because the stroke tempo should be very high and the knee bend extra deep. This is probably the toughest of all the stroke types to perform well and safely. This is an optional stroke and should be used by skiers who are very comfortable with it. Therefore, we have chosen not to cover it in any further depth in this section or in the section on stroke transitions. Experiment with it if you like, but classify it in the realm of expert skiers who need a stroke that can be performed at the highest possible speeds.

The idea of all these variations is to use quick tempo, moderate to deep knee bend, a low recovery (i.e., recover the ski by pulling the knee to the chest), and a quick, shortened poling motion that will end without the traditional high follow-through. Because both feet are out of the tracks at all times with symmetrical skating, the glide on either ski is never directly parallel to the line of travel. If you glide too long on either ski, you will be wasting time traveling back and forth across the intended line of travel. Keep side-to-side travel to a minimum by keeping the tempo high and striving to keep your skis as parallel as possible to the line of travel.

Symmetry and Balance. SVS requires more confidence and balance than any other stroke type. It is important to remember that any extra upper body movement will throw you off balance. Stroke symmetry (i.e., keeping the left push/pole equal to the right) is all that allows you to maintain control of this stroke. Once you lose control, you end up expending more energy in recovery and in struggling to maintain your balance than you are expending to propel yourself down the track.

Stay loose and relaxed. Keeping your upper body very quiet and very small in its motions (remember Mack?) will allow you to stay in control and to keep all stokes equal. This is another reason for keeping whatever accelerating you want to do under control. If you accelerate too fast, you sacrifice your symmetry and therefore your efficiency. Losing symmetry in this stroke means disaster.

SVS was the stroke most used on the 1986 World Cup circuit. Skiers are finding that, with practice, this difficult stroke can become a smooth, relaxed stroke that is useful on all parts of the course. What they have done is to make this a "dynamic" stroke, meaning that you never allow your joints to sit too long in any one position. Using this stroke with a slow tempo or hitches in the stroke where you sit too long on a bent knee (resulting in static muscle activity) will kill your legs and could damage your knees.

The key to using SVS successfully is to keep all your motions fluid, allowing yourself to flow through and between strokes as if each stroke were a wave motion. This will take a lot of practice. The SVS stroke is discussed further later in this chapter, particularly in the section on poling.

Marathon Skate

The marathon skate is the stroke that started it all. Coaches and magazines have criticized the marathon as no longer being a useful technique. We see this criticism as an example of not knowing how to use a perfectly good stroke, under the proper conditions, at the proper time.

No single skating stroke is well suited for all conditions and every situation. The fact that the marathon lends itself well to low tempo, deep knee bend, power poling, and usefulness at high speeds dictates that there is a right and wrong time and place to use this stroke. It was first used very successfully on the marathon circuit where there are fewer hills and more extensive flats. Now skiers on the World Cup circuit are ignoring marathon because it is not a good stroke to use on uphills. Use a stroke where its strengths suggest and find another stroke to take its place in situations where its weaknesses would be a hindrance. You must know the strengths and weaknesses of every stroke type before deciding where to use each stroke on the course.

Different Strokes, Different Tempos. Today's coaches will tell you that the ability to maintain high stroke tempo is a key factor in racing success. Some stroke types lend themselves to higher stroke tempos. These strokes should be employed under any conditions in which your glide may be inhibited, such as bad track, deep snow, extreme cold or wind, or any uphill that would break your momentum. The key to skating is to maintain momentum, and the way to do that is to rely more on push and less on glide, especially under conditions in which the glide is inhibited. By keeping the stroke tempo high, you are more likely to avoid the deceleration that results from gliding too long.

On the other hand, there are parts of every course where maintaining your speed is less difficult, such as on downhills or long flat runouts following a downhill. In these areas you will be traveling at such a high rate of speed that a high tempo stroke would be more likely to throw you off balance and inhibit your glide. In these situations you should turn to a power stroke, like the marathon skate.

Because you'll be performing the marathon stride at high speeds, the balance factor becomes critical. The marathon is the stroke that results in the most spectacular head-plant accidents, so you'll want to be careful about initiating any quick moves before you have achieved proper balance. Remember to prepare yourself for each stroke by setting your shoulders and hips squarely perpendicular to the line of travel. Any twisting will create torque and resistance on the gliding ski as well as increase the chance of slipping with the pushing ski. Furthermore, if the hip falls behind during the stroke, then the push will be directed to the rear. By now you should know that this is not the desired situation. With this in mind, we can begin to discuss the stroke itself.

From a starting position with both feet in the tracks, the marathon begins by shifting your weight entirely onto the left foot (which will become the gliding ski) and lifting the right ski out of the track, angling it slightly outward (the greater the speed, the lower the angle). The trick now is to get your weight back onto the pushing ski before the push can actually begin. This is done by bending the knees (while the poles are planted) and shifting the weight onto the pushing ski, meaning that the pushing leg is fully bent when the ski first makes contact with the snow. Now a normal stroke and weight transfer can commence, and recovery will be accomplished by merely standing on the new gliding ski before preparing for the next push. It is at this time during the recovery phase that you must avoid twisting your hips and upper body. Twisting your hips can easily occur when you are always pushing with the same foot, so make a point to keep your hips square.

You must also avoid developing one strong side and one weak side by always pushing with the same leg. Mix up your marathon strokes in both training and racing to prevent this situation. You'll need to know how to marathon skate to both sides for negotiating turns anyway.

Three-Point Contact.   Whereas symmetrical skating employs a skiing rhythm (the combination of poling and skating) similar to that of the conventional diagonal stride, the marathon and asymmetrical v-skate techniques yield best results when a technique described as *three-point contact* is used. By three-point contact, we mean that both pole tips and the pushing ski will all make contact with the snow simultaneously at the beginning of each stroke. This is easiest to practice with the marathon, and that is why we are covering it first.

To get the feel of three-point contact, stand up with your poles in your hands. Stand on your left foot, with both pole tips lifted off the floor, as though you were gliding on skis with your left foot in the track and were about to initiate a marathon push with your right foot. The way to begin the push is by making three-point contact. Plant both poles and your pushing (right) foot at the same moment. By skiing in this manner, you use your poles to supply momentum during the moment while you are building up pressure on the pushing ski. This is one of many skating techniques designed to maintain momentum in your skating.

Changing Sides.   To be able to go between sides of the marathon stroke, you'll need a transition stroke. The simplest transition we can recommend is to break the two marathon strokes with a big, strong double-pole. Then on the next stroke (on the new side) you can pull the new pushing foot out of the tracks to begin pushing on the new side. Always practice the marathon stroke on both sides (i.e., with both the right and left legs) to avoid developing a strong side and a weak side.

Weaknesses.   Until now we have been describing marathon skating as it applies to your skis in the tracks, and this points out the obvious weakness inherent in the stroke: It is less effective and more difficult to perform in the absence of tracks. Luckily, the places on a course where you are most likely to use the marathon (i.e., downhills and high-speed flats) usually have not had the tracks obliterated by the skiers ahead of you. If the tracks have been obliterated, then your best bet might be to abandon the marathon in favor of one of the other stroke types that works well without tracks, most likely a symmetrical v-skate.

Marathon Variations.   There are two variations on the marathon skate, which make it one of the more versatile strokes (in the presence of tracks). These are the *marathon tuck* and the *marathon skate turn*.

The marathon tuck is a transition stroke that a racer would use on a downhill to go from a tuck position into the marathon stride. This is the skating maneuver that is performend at the highest speeds and is performed without using the poles at all. At such high speeds, a backward thrust with the poles would add nothing to your speed and would probably throw you off balance. This stroke is initiated from a gliding tuck position by shifting the weight onto the chosen gliding ski, while maintaining a deep tuck, and picking up the free ski out of the track. It will be set down outside of and parallel to the track. You'll give a long, powerful push from the tuck position, while still keeping the poles tucked under your arms.

There is no "stand up" in the recovery; instead, you recover the pushing ski by bringing that knee up almost to your chest (still in a downhill tuck) before carefully placing it back down on the snow to begin another push. We'll talk more about this in the section on transitions.

Outside Marathon Turn. The other variation of the marathon skate is a cornering technique. In order to power around a turn on a course, you must skate through it. The stroke you'll be using here is a marathon, supplying the power with the pushing foot, while the gliding ski steers you around the curve.

The decision you will have to make on each curve is on which side of the track to push, that is, the inside or the outside of the curve. For most skiers this decision is a matter of personal preference. For a skier who prefers strokes that allow enough time for a standing transition, however, better use would be made of pushing to the *outside*. A stroke to the outside is more conducive to a long power stroke, fully built up and performed from a deep knee bend. A skier pushing to the outside must always be careful not to let the push be directed to the rear. Extra care must be taken to prevent this because the track itself is pulling you away from the original direction of the push.

This is a situation in which the skier must be thinking of trying to push forward. One way to accomplish this is to lift the glide ski slightly off the snow with each pushing stroke and return it to the track with the secondary weight transfer. Many of the

quicker "power skiers" have had great success with
this "light glide" technique, especially Maurilio Dezolt
of the Italian men's team. This technique forces the
skier's weight back on the rear of the skis, thus forcing
the pushing ski to travel forward rather than fall
behind.

Inside Marathon Turn. Racers are now beginning
to experiment with pushing to the inside of a turn because it seems to work better at lower speeds with
high tempo strokes in which no "stand-up recovery" is
used. By keeping the same degree of knee bend between strokes, your stroke turnover rate can be kept
higher. You are no longer wasting time standing up to
recover the free ski between each stroke. By pushing
with the marathon stroke to the inside of the curve,
your pushing ski is automatically directed forward by
the tracks, thus pulling you around to meet the direction of push. As a result, there is not enough time for a
long, powerful stroke to be used, so maintain the knee
bend between strokes and increase the tempo.

We do not recommend using an Italian step with
this inside marathon turn because part of the advantage of this type of stroke is that the push itself is
actually creating more pressure against centrifugal
force in the gliding track. This is something you will
feel when you try it, and picking up the gliding ski
would only spoil this advantage.

Changing Tracks. The only topic left to cover on
the marathon skate is the practice that many skiers
have taken up of changing track sides. What this
means is that skiers are setting their right ski in the
left track and pushing with the left ski out in the
"clean" snow. Theoretically, this doesn't sound like a
bad idea; not having to cross tracks with each push
would provide more secure footing for the pushing ski.
For all but the most elite skiers, however, we feel this
is a waste of time. More time is probably lost in
continually changing tracks (thus surrendering pre-
cious momentum) and in getting up from falls caused
by too many off-balance track changes than is actually
gained from having a better piece of snow on which to
push. Remember where and how to use the marathon
stride, and this stroke will serve you well.

Asymmetrical V-Skate

The asymmetrical v-skate (AVS) is the most commonly used stroke on uphills, but it has few advantages (other than as a rest stroke) on other parts of the course. This stroke works exactly as its name implies. AVS involves pushing alternately with both skis but utilizing a "strong side" (combining a skate with a double-pole) and a "weak side" (a skating stroke performed while the poles recover to the starting position), thus leaving an asymmetrical "V" pattern in the snow. In other words, with AVS you pole on the strong side and recover on the weak side (see Figure 3.3).

Three-Point Contact.   As with the marathon, three-point contact will be used to dictate the rhythm of the AVS poling motion. The easiest way to learn this poling rhythm is on a pair of roller skis or roller skates. To get the feel for the coordination between legs and arms, stand on your roller skates with poles in your hands and start walking forward, planting your

Figure 3.3 Excellent AVS stagger-pole technique is displayed by Marko Mehtonen of Fi land as he churns up a hill during the 1986 World Junior Champi nships in Lake Placid, New York. Notice how he drives the free leg for ard and gets his upper body weight over the poles without allowin his feet to drop behind his hips.

poles at the same moment that you step down on your right foot. As you walk more quickly, your skates will begin to roll and you will naturally assume the correct poling rhythm. Be sure to learn this three-point technique on both sides. By the time you get on the snow, it will be second nature to you.

The reason for using this poling rhythm with AVS is that it will provide power while your body weight is still loading up the next pushing stroke. Because AVS will probably become your favorite climbing stroke, it makes sense to have as little dead time as possible for the skis to run out of glide. Three-point contact allows you to keep a very high stroke tempo without losing your balance and also provides you with a rhythm that keeps at least one part of your body involved in maintaining momentum at all times.

AVS is like a marathon stride with an extra push. It depends less on glide and more on push to maintain speed. For that reason it is most useful on uphills or during bad track or bad weather conditions as a substitute for the marathon. The nature of the AVS stroke lends itself best to use with a moderate to quick stroke tempo. But in situations where the hill you are climbing is so steep that even a moderate tempo becomes a chore, you must be ready to abandon this stroke in favor of one that works more efficiently at slow speeds. In these situations you must utilize a stroke that can maintain a higher tempo and incorporates a "low" recovery and a pole push with each skating stroke to maintain momentum.

Why Not Always Use AVS? Many skiers have begun using AVS almost exclusively during training and races, on all parts of the course, because it is such an easy and comfortable stroke. We feel that this is an error. No single stroke can serve you best on all parts of the course. AVS can be very useful on hills and will probably become your favorite "climbing gear," but some hills or parts of hills will call for a stroke that can be performed more efficiently at even higher tempos. Trying to bull your way through by putting more power into each stroke, as opposed to switching to another stroke and a higher tempo, is like bicycling up a hill in a gear that is too big. You go progressively slower and build up lactic acid faster. Knowing when

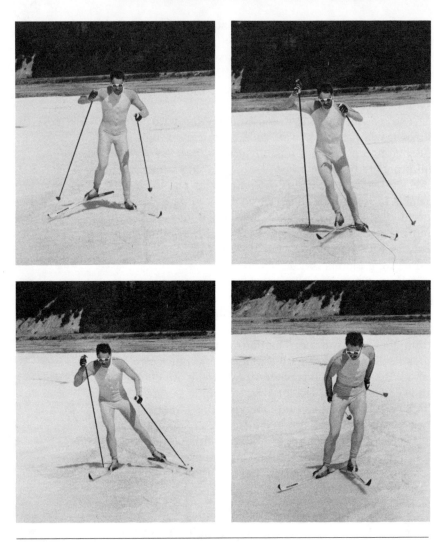

Figure 3.4 This series of photos shows Audun Endestad performing an asymmetrical v-skate stroke with a stagger-poling motion. Notice in Frame 2 how he leads with his right hip and sets the gliding ski down slightly on the outside edge. His pushing foot maintains almost constant heel contact with the ski.

to "switch gears" on a hill can only come with experience. Knowing all the strokes and being able to perform them all effectively is the first step toward making those decisions intelligently (see Figure 3.4).

Common Mistakes. The two most common mistakes associated with AVS are overuse and "sleeping" through the weak-side push. By "overuse" we mean that many skiers use this stroke almost exclusively in all conditions and on all parts of the course. No single skating stroke is optimal for all conditions and situations, and using only AVS, which could arguably be considered the most versatile stroke, simply means that you will be losing seconds every time you use it at a point on the course where another stroke type would be more effective.

"Sleeping" is another problem encountered in trying to master the AVS. Sleeping is the habit people have of giving a big push on the strong side and pushing almost not at all on the weak side. The whole idea of AVS is to maintain more momentum by more consistently applying force to the snow. If you sleep through the weak side, you are defeating this purpose and allowing your speed a chance to run out.

AVS is a two-sided stroke, and a strong skating push should be used on both sides. The double-pole is the only thing making one side stronger than the other. In fact, for some skiers the actual skating stroke of the weak side could be stronger than the skating stroke of the strong side. This is a result of the nature of the stroke, which dictates that the skier is automatically "loaded" on the weak side. This happens because the end of the strong-side push leaves you already gliding on a bent knee before the weak-side push begins (preloaded). The push occurs from this preloaded position (without standing up to recover), whereas a standing recovery is required before the strong-side push to allow time for the poles to recover to the ready position.

AVS Variations.   The primary variation that is used (and overused) with AVS is called a *stagger-pole*. The stagger-pole is basically a double-poling motion, but instead of planting both poles at once, one is planted slightly before the other. Skiers find this useful as a change of pace or as a rest stroke, but it is usually misused as a compensation for poles that are too long (an increasingly common mistake) (see Figure 3.5).

Incline Stagger-Pole.   The best application of the stagger-pole is on uphills that lean slightly to one side, where the skier must traverse across an incline using an uphill foot and a downhill foot. In a situation such as this, the skier should use a stagger-pole, leading

Figure 3.5 Audun Endestad shows excellent technique performing an asymmetrical v-skate stroke with a stagger-poling motion. Notice in Frames 2 and 3 how his pushing foot never falls behind his hips, even though he completely collapsed his upper body weight onto the poles.

with the uphill arm (i.e., planting that pole first), and always keep the strong-side push (with the double-pole) on the side where the ski must glide up the incline. This will allow the weak-side push (without the double-pole) to direct itself slightly down the incline,

losing as little momentum as possible while the poles
are recovering.

If you were to reverse this situation and double-
pole in conjunction with the downhill side push, the
weak-side push would have to climb back up the slope
without the aid of the poling motion, thus losing pre-
cious momentum. In other words, you must learn to
perform this stagger-pole variation on both sides (i.e.,
be able to lead with either hand) because sometimes
the hill will slope the wrong way and you will have the
opportunity to gain time on your competitors. You will
be able to do so if you have complete command of the
stagger-poling technique.

Angle of Push

This section pertains to all skating strokes. What
we are dealing with is the fact as a skier goes slower,
gaining momentum while pushing out to the side becomes increasingly difficult. The solution to this
problem is not to allow your skis to push back but
rather to increase the angle between your skis (i.e.,
widen the "v"). Even in this situation you must keep
trying to direct your pushes straight out to the side.
You should think of pushing the skis out toward the
tips with each stroke. Concentrate on forcing each ski
to glide forward with each stroke, maintaining heel
contact as long as possible on each stroke.

This is possible, even on steep uphills, by sitting
back and weighting the tails of the skis. It is impera-
tive that you continue to think of letting the skis glide
and not allow yourself to roll the ski over too far on its
edge. Doing so would kill your glide, force you to push
back, and turn your stroke into a herringbone. You
can practically ski up a mountainside by sitting back
far enough and being patient enough to let your skis
glide. The glide may be only a few centimeters, but
maintaining momentum is the name of the game, and
even minimal glide is worth hanging on to. If you get
too slow to glide, you can always resort to the herringbone (see Figure 3.6).

All you need to remember is that the angle of push
(i.e., the "v" angle between your skis) will increase as
your speed decreases (an inverse relationship). This
does not imply that you are pushing back but only

Figure 3.6 Josh Thompson of the U.S. Biathlon Team working to gain speed while leaving the shooting area. His skating technique is excellent at these low speeds. He doesn't even have a complete hold on his poles yet. Notice how his body is centered and relaxed even under the stress of acceleration. His pushing foot still maintains complete contact with the ski. The wide angle of his skis is a result of the low rate of speed.

that you are not attempting to cover as much forward ground with each stroke as if you were traveling faster.

Riding a Flat Ski. We would all probably agree that
a ski will glide more easily if it is sitting flat on the
snow as opposed to being turned on its edge. For this
reason trying to ride a flat ski at all times has often
been recommended. Coaches have suggested that skiers
attempt to set down the gliding foot as flat as possible
with each new stroke. This is another case where the
intention is right, but the instruction is incomplete.

Most of us have difficulty keeping our skis tracking
properly on hard packed snow when we are trying to
set it down flat each time. Trying to keep the glide ski
so flat also causes most beginners to ski with their feet
too far apart to be effective. If you watch the best
skiers, you will see that they set down the glide ski
slightly on the outside edge and quickly roll it over
onto the flat, where the load-up will occur. At first this
approach may cause a lot of falls. Nevertheless, we
advocate this style because it allows you to keep your
feet directly under you and does not significantly
reduce the time you spend gliding on a flat ski.

On the ice, speed skaters are free to lean far out on
the outside edge at the beginning of each glide. On
skis, however the outside edge seems to grab the
snow, propelling athletes off into the woods. This is
the one part of skating technique that will cause many
falls in beginners. You must, however, develop the
confidence to keep your feet together during skating
strokes. After a little practice this element of technique, like all the others, will become second nature to
you.

Poling

It's finally time to tie all these skating techniques
into a fluid system, and the way that happens is
through properly coordinated poling. We mentioned
earlier how the poling motion used in conjunction with
skating is more abbreviated than a conventional
double-pole. This does not mean, however, that it
should be less effective.

The tricky part of combining skating and poling is
being able to sit back on your skis at the proper moment of the push while still allowing your upper body

Figure 3.7 In this poling sequence notice how the weight of the upper body collapses onto the poles without allowing the feet to drop behind the hips.

to get on top of the poles to make the pole stroke more effective. Beginning skaters often do one or the other; they either rely on the poles almost exclusively and just put their feet through the skating motions, or else they skate with the feet only while their arms add nothing more than rhythm. Balance and confidence are most often the determining factors here, and learning a good, accurate poling motion early in your development as a skater will keep you from developing any of these bad habits (see Figure 3.7).

Many skiers have acquired the elements of proper technique, but they put those elements together like a "breakdancer," with each movement isolated from every other. The key to making skating work for you lies in making each stroke smooth and dynamic, and mastering this does not come quickly or easily.

There are essentially two poling rhythms that work best with skating strokes: a "conventional" rhythm and a "three-point" rhythm. Three-point contact has already been described earlier in this chapter in the section on the asymmetrical v-skate. We described the type of poling rhythm to use, planting the poles at the same time the pushing ski contacts the snow (at the very beginning of the load-up). A conventional rhythm, on the other hand, has a slightly different feel to it, and one that you should already be fairly comfortable with. It is the same rhythm used in the diagonal stride of conventional skiing.

In a conventional poling rhythm, such as you would use with any of the SVS strokes, you are already standing on the pushing foot when you go to load it up (unlike in a marathon stroke or AVS, where you step onto the foot at the moment the load-up begins). This means that in AVS the poling will be in its power phase while the stroke is loading up, whereas in SVS the power phase of both the poling and the skating strokes will happen simultaneously (and the arms and legs will gain full extension at the same time).

Poling Basics.   The following items are basic to all poling done in conjunction with skating strokes:

1. Plant the poles ahead of the ski bindings and as close to the ski as possible. If after a fair amount of practice you still find it difficult to get a close pole plant, try using some shorter poles for a while.
2. Poling should always be done with the weight of the upper body, but not with the full "bow" used in conventional double-poling. Poles should be planted with the elbows cocked. The weight will be transferred through the poles by lowering the body weight, not by stretching forward, and using the shoulders as a lever (as in a conventional double-pole).

3. Your arms will be bent through much of the poling motion, especially as the grips pass by your hips. A low, unexaggerated follow-through is recommended. When the poles have finished the power phase after passing the hips, you should begin to ease off and begin the recovery. Keep your poling motions quick and don't worry about trying to power each one.

4. If you initiate your poling from too upright a body position, you may be forcing your weight onto your toes. You must extend your body weight out over the poles at the beginning of each stroke but do so without allowing the weight on your feet to concentrate on the toes. This sounds impossible, but it can be achieved with practice and concentration.

5. If you allow yourself to make a full "bow" at the end of the poling motion, you will rock your weight forward onto the toes. This will cause the skating stroke to scoot away from you, shortening the stroke and making recovery more difficult. Your upper body must collapse its weight onto the poles but do so without bending so much at the hips so that the weight on the feet is thrown forward.

6. There are no stopping points or "poses" in good skating technique. Poling is part of this dynamic nature of the stroke. Poling strokes should flow as smoothly as possible, from one into the next, with no breaks. This means that you will no longer feel a big "heave" in your poling. Your poling stroke should still be powerful but should disappear into the wave-like motion of the skating stroke as a whole.

7. As snow conditions become slower, poling technique becomes more important. This is because poling can lift the skis when they are sinking and the skating is becoming less effective. Practice your poling until you can comfortably maintain very high tempos for these situations without spoiling your rhythm or throwing off your balance.

Stroke
Transitions

4

Knowing how to skate all the strokes correctly will make you a better skier, but knowing where on a course to use each type of stroke and how to move quickly and smoothly from one type to another is what will make you fast. You already know that the key to success in skating is maintaining momentum. One of the areas where speed can be lost is in sloppy transitions that waste time or kill momentum while moving from one stroke type to another.

What we hope to establish in this chapter is a system that will help you to know which stroke to use, when to switch strokes, exactly how to move through the transition, and which stroke to use next. There should never be a question as to which stroke type to change to for any given circumstance. Indecision or hesitation always wastes time. Our goal is to take the randomness out of choosing the type of stroke. You have already been told where each type of stroke is most useful, so let's explore exactly how to get from one type to another.

Why Change Strokes?

You will need to make stroke transitions for a combination of reasons. Either the terrain will have changed or the skier will need to "shift gears" up or down. In other words, transitions are dictated by the combined elements of the course and the athlete's comfort level.

You must also realize that transitions always occur through the tempo of the stroke. For example, you would never change from a marathon stroke directly to SVS because their optimal stroke tempos are vastly

different. A transition will always occur to the stroke of
the next higher or next lower tempo capability, without skipping any transition phases. Just as you
wouldn't want to move from first to fourth gear on
your new car, you cannot make a transition from a
low-tempo skating stroke to a very high-tempo skating
stroke (see Figure 4.1).

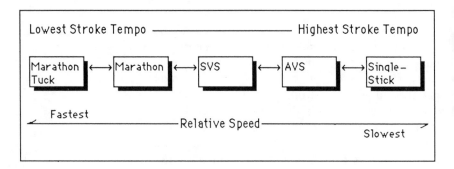

Figure 4.1 Stroke transitions.

This may mean that you will make only one or two
pushes using a particular stroke type after a transition
before moving on to the next transition, but developing
this type of system will take all the guesswork and
indecision out of your skiing. The less severe break in
stroke tempo and the energy saved will enable you to
maintain more speed and momentum.

The Transitions Explained

We have identified five different transitions that we
believe are necessary in any skier's repertoire. Other
stroke transitions are possible, most including SVS
without poles, but the five following transitions are
enough for almost any skier, and there is no need to
confuse the issue by catering to everyone's personal
preferences.

1. Downhill tuck to marathon tuck (highest speed,
   lowest tempo)
2. Marathon tuck to marathon

3. Marathon to SVS
4. SVS to AVS
5. AVS to SVS single-stick (lowest speed, highest tempo)

In describing these transitions, we will discuss each both ways: from fast to slow (skier slowing down) and from slow to fast (skier speeding up).

Transition One

Transition One goes between the marathon tuck and a downhill tuck.

Fast to Slow: Tuck to Marathon Tuck. This is where the worst falls happen. If you ever watch a race, stand where this transition is being used and take a count of the head-plants. Those people who fell were not the daring or crazy skiers; rather they were the tentative skiers who did not commit totally to the transition.

Here's the problem. A skier in a downhill tuck, at full speed, is asked to pick one foot up out of the track and push it out to the side to gain even more speed. What most skiers neglect, and what would have prevented disaster, is to shift the weight completely to the gliding ski (i.e., the one still in the track) before ever picking up the ski they intend to push with. Once that weight shift is complete, the pushing ski can then be placed outside the track, nearly parallel to it (remember the high rate of speed you are carrying), and the weight will then be transferred to the pushing foot to begin the stroke.

Once the push has been loaded and the stroke is complete, the stroke will end by shifting the weight back to the standing leg. In recovering that ski, however, you will not be standing up. Stay in the tuck and recover it slowly by bringing the knee to the chest. And keep your toes up! A downhill tuck at 40 kilometers per hour is no time to catch a tip. Remember that a marathon tuck is a high speed maneuver, so keep the tempo slow and power each stroke from a deeply bent knee.

If you are not confident or not willing to commit fully to this transition, then don't use it or you risk becoming just another statistic. This transition does supply a marked increase in speed and will give you an advantage during a race, but all these transitions have one thing in common: They all pose potential for falls. If you feel less than confident, hang on to the speed you've got and don't risk losing it to an unexpected spill.

Slow to Fast: Marathon Tuck to Downhill Tuck. This transition would be used when speed is building on a downhill. Often, soon after cresting a hill and starting down, it does you some good to give a few powerful marathon tuck strokes before settling down into your downhill tuck. The only tip we can give you is to use marathon tuck pushes until you feel that you may lose your balance due to the increased speed. At that point regroup the pushing ski, keeping your toes up to avoid catching a tip, and set it back in the track. This is the point where you could also use SVS with no poling. It is an excellent way to build speed after having crested a hill. This is a tough stroke requiring superb balance and greater than average courage when speed is increasing.

You will generally ride out the tuck until you begin slowing down again. Then it is time to switch back to a marathon tuck. This marathon tuck to downhill tuck transition could be skipped entirely if you never feel off balance performing a marathon tuck. Why just glide down a hill when you can skate down it?

Transition Two

Transition Two goes between the marathon tuck and the marathon.

Fast to Slow: Marathon Tuck to Marathon. You have used the marathon tuck to get you moving out of your downhill tuck, but if you try to keep practicing that stroke using deep knee bend and no poles across the flat, your thighs will probably catch fire. This is the time to move into the marathon skate.

All this transition requires is, after increasing the tempo of the marathon tuck that you have been using, performing a normal stand-up recovery, followed by a regular marathon stride utilizing a full marathon double-pole. This is the easiest of the transitions. Don't waste speed by doing any double-poling at this point. You are probably going too fast for it to do any good.

Slow to Fast: Marathon to Marathon Tuck. As speed increases after cresting a hill and starting down, you may use a few marathon strokes on the downside. These will lead into one or two marathon tuck strokes before settling into a tuck. The easiest way to accomplish that transition is to leave out the standing recovery at the end of the strongest marathon stroke. Don't let up just before the transition. Stay in a low knee bend and let the poles fold up under your arms. Now make one or two marathon tuck strokes and move into the downhill tuck at full speed.

Never let a downhill be fully responsible for your speed increases. Skate over the top and down the other side before settling into your tuck out of necessity. If you feel confident, skate down the whole other side.

Transition Three

Transition Three goes between symmetrical v-skating and the marathon (see Figure 4.2).

Fast to Slow: Marathon to SVS. This transition should be used when your speed has begun to die after a long, fast flat. The key to the switch is to increase energy output and stroke tempo up to and through the

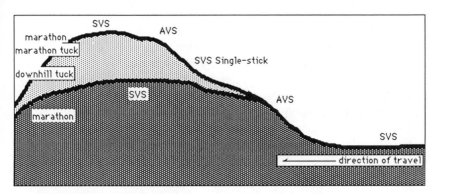

Figure 4.2 Stroke transitions.

actual transition, just as you would stand up to pedal before and after shifting gears on a bicycle. In this way less momentum will be lost in the struggling and hesitating of the stroke change.

Problems with the Transition.   There is one problem with this transition. Complications could arise due to the presence of tracks. If the skiers before you have not obliterated the tracks, your gliding ski will be stuck in the track when it comes time for the transition. When dealing with that possibility, the "Italian step" will come in handy. If you are already lifting the gliding ski slightly with each push, then getting that ski out of the tracks will be easier when the time comes to make the transition. If the tracks have been erased, then it will be best to maintain glide contact as much as possible.

As this transition occurs, you will merely lift the gliding ski out of the tracks during the last marathon stroke and set it down outside and almost parallel to the tracks to begin the first SVS stroke. Of course, your poles must have recovered quickly to begin the SVS at this point. The following step-by-step progression may make this transition easier to understand:

1. Switch sides of marathon skating four to six strokes before the transition. Increase tempo and Italian-step in the tracks.
2. Begin the transition midway through the marathon push by lifting the glide ski out of the track and setting it down across the track at an angle in proportion to present rate of speed. Keep the angle low, as close to parallel as possible. Don't take your time here. Be prepared to make the transition quickly and decisively. Pole recovery after the last marathon push must be very quick. Remember that you must have the poles ready to plant for the first SVS stroke immediately after you have picked up your ski out of the tracks.
3. In SVS keep up accelerated tempo for at least four strokes after the transition to prevent further loss of momentum.

Slow to Fast: SVS to Marathon. This is an easy transition to use when your speed is increasing to the point at which SVS becomes a little clumsy. After a few quick strokes, simply plant one leg back in the track and keep the strong-side leg active in the marathon skate.

Transition Four

Transition Four goes between SVS and AVS. Two things will always happen in this transition, whether it goes from fast to slow or from slow to fast. Transition Four will ignore tracks entirely, and it will require a *change-up*, an interim poling motion to allow for a totally new poling tempo.

Fast to Slow: SVS to AVS. This is the first transition to use when your momentum begins to die on an uphill. When you are losing speed, it is best to switch to a stroke type that involves quicker stroke tempo and more consistent poling that depends more on push and less on glide. You will be able to determine that point only after lots of time experimenting on your skis. Suffice it to say that skiers should not feel they are "laboring" (i.e., having to think about pushing harder) in a particular stroke. On a ten-speed bicycle, your gear choice should change before your cadence, or effort, is significantly affected. Use this same idea in making stroke choices on skis.

All that is required to move smoothly from SVS to AVS is a slight increase in stroke tempo and a change in poling motion. This entails switching from a double-pole on each stroke (with SVS) to a strong-side/weak-side situation (with AVS). All you need to do is pick up the tempo slightly and pick a stroke to begin the quick recovery of the poles, every other stroke, which will allow you to begin the different, three-point contact rhythm. This means that you will need to perform the last SVS stroke without poling so that you will be ready to plant the poles and skating ski simultaneously when you begin AVS.

Be prepared for this transition ahead of time. Don't waste time and momentum by throwing in too many skating strokes with no poling. You are crawling up a steep hill, and this is no time to be sacrificing momentum due to slow acting or indecision. Execute the transition as quickly as possible and return to the task of gaining a little speed where you can.

Slow to Fast: AVS to SVS. If you have used AVS to get over the top of a hill, this is the first transition to use when starting down the other side. As your speed increases, you will reach a point where increasing your tempo with AVS becomes difficult. At that point all you need to do is to speed up one of your pole recoveries and include poling on what was the weak side.

Remember to increase the tempo of your strokes slightly before the transition, even though the tempo you'll be using in SVS will be somewhat slower than with AVS. This increase is made to ensure that as little momentum as possible is lost during the transition. The speed you are carrrying on the hill will very likely determine that you need to move quickly out of SVS and into a higher speed stroke such as a marathon.

Some skiers choose to skip this transition by taking AVS directly into a marathon. We think it's best to always keep all your strokes in order and to practice them that way so that during a race there will never be any question as to which stroke comes next. But transitions that occur on the downside of a hill are highly individualized. If you devise systems of your own that feel more comfortable, stick with them. Many skiers like to experiment with SVS without poling on downhills. For those of you with better than average balance and brave hearts, good luck and more power to you!

Transition Five

Transition Five goes between AVS and SVS single-stick. This is the transition that always occurs at the lowest speeds. Changing from single-stick to herringbone takes place at a lower speed but does not involve glide, so we do not include it as a transition.

Fast to Slow: AVS to SVS Single-Stick. If you are going slow enough to need this transition, then you can't afford to lose any more time or speed. Thus smoothness and directness of action are very important. All you'll be doing is increasing the stroke tempo and beginning a "diagonal" or single-stick poling motion. To accomplish the change in poling motion, you'll pick a double-pole sequence, but rather than recover both poles for a double-pole you'll allow one pole to stay ahead while the other pushes in conjunction with the leg on its opposite side.

You may need to experiment with this particular transition. We recommend finding the system that works best for you, learning to do it quickly, and then doing it exactly the same way every time.

Slow to Fast: Single-Stick to AVS. This transition requires a change-up, as in switching from a conventional diagonal stride to a double-pole. Because your speed is increasing, you will be able to afford to waste a stroke and take the time to do one skating stroke without poling while both poles are traveling forward to prepare for the new double-poling motion. Often the AVS strokes that follow this transition will not last more than a few seconds before requiring that you switch to SVS. We suggest practicing this transition as a series of three: from single-stick, to AVS, to SVS.

A Transition Checklist

You should remember the following hints relating to stroke choice, skating conditions, and transitions in all skating situations:

1. Low speed requires high stroke tempo. Low skiing speed is best dealt with by increasing the tempo of the stroke initially and, if necessary, using a transition to another stroke type that is more conducive to use at slower speeds. Select another stroke type that relies more on push and less on glide.
2. High speed requires low stroke tempo. When already carrying a lot of speed, try to maintain your speed by using a deeper knee bend than normal and powering each stroke. Keeping your stroke

tempo too high at such a high speed may only serve to throw you off balance.

3. Bad conditions spoil your glide. Treat bad conditions as though you were on a slight, constant uphill. Depend more on increased tempo and emphasize push over glide.

4. Uphills can be considered bad conditions and should be dealt with the same way.

5. Increase your stroke tempo before any transition. This will help to maintain the momentum you may have lost in hesitating to change stroke types. It keeps "dead time" to a minimum.

6. When you want to increase your tempo, do it with your poles first. Your legs are going to follow your arms (not vice versa), so generate a new tempo by rushing your poling slightly.

7. Don't skip transition phases. Transitions must be made to the stroke of the next highest or next lowest tempo capability and not to any other. This will help to keep you organized. Eventually, you won't need to consciously think about which stroke to use next; it will just come naturally in long, continuous strings of transitions (with fewer breaks in tempo and momentum).

8. There should be no pauses during transitions. The transition from one stroke type to another should be so well connected that it is practically invisible.

9. Keep your head up when you ski. Even if you become proficient enough to do all the transitions in your sleep, you won't be able to do them properly if you fail to see that the need for one is coming up. Look down the track and plan your transitions in advance. Being forced into a transition you did not expect will only cause you to pause and regroup. That's just wasting time.

10. Practice stringing your transitions together. Often you will need to use a particular stroke for only one or two pushes before moving into another transition. Perhaps all five transitions will be included within 15-20 strokes. If you don't practice these situations in advance, you can't be on top of the situation when it counts.

11. Transitions on an uphill should happen slightly before you need them. If you wait until you really

need a different stroke tempo, then you will be losing too much momentum in the transition itself. Plan ahead. "Shift gears" before your body really begins to labor.

The main idea we are trying to get across in this chapter is that skiers waste a lot of time when switching from one stroke type to another. We have tried to provide a system for avoiding the delays that will rob you of momentum. If you don't like our systems, devise one of your own. No matter what, find a way to maintain your momentum through the transitions.

Training as a Skating Skier

5

One of the problems facing skiers new to skating is that skating places different demands on your body and new demands on how you must train. Up until the use of skating techniques became widespread, cross-country skiing had been primarily an endurance event. Skating is much more explosive and energy-sapping than conventional skiing, and this has led to some new ideas about how to train for cross-country skiing.

Although endurance is no longer the primary physiological factor for success in competitive skiing, all good skiers need adequate endurance. Skiers are no longer looking at their events as something to merely survive. Skiers are now seeking *speed* over the snow. This attitude is resulting in some basic changes in the workouts skiers are doing and the ways in which skiers are constructing and arranging their workout programs. In the search for speed and strength, many old ideas about training, both dryland and on snow, are being reevaluated and improved. This chapter will discuss these new ideas and how to accommodate them in your program.

First we must define the basic types of workouts that will constitute any complete program. We have classified the following seven workout types:

1. Endurance workouts
2. Interval workouts
3. Tempo workouts
4. Speed/sprint workouts
5. Strength workouts
6. Technical workouts
7. Recreation/coordination workouts

Figure 5.1 A well-organized and diverse dryland training program will be certain to improve your cross-country skating performance next winter.

Endurance Training

Speed may be what racers are seeking, but in the final analysis cross-country races are still distance events. Skiers still need ongoing endurance training to be properly prepared for cross-country competition. Speed and strength are required to win races today, but conditioning for speed and strength cannot be achieved without a year-round training program that is based on endurance training.

Endurance training is what you are doing any time you raise your heart rate above normal and maintain that level of activity for more than a couple of minutes. As you can see, that covers a wide range of training activities. Almost any type of continuous training, from weight lifting to distance running, will improve an athlete's endurance. The important thing is to determine what type of workout and what intensity best suit your needs in improving your capabilities as an endurance athlete.

You can train for endurance at many different levels and intensities, from a 15-minute run to a 5-hour bike ride and on every type of training apparatus from skis to slideboards and weight machines. What has changed in training for cross-country skiing is that with the advent of skating, athletes have a greater need to be able to maintain more explosive muscular activity over a long period of time. Only a few sports, such as speed skating and rowing, require this unique combination of strength and endurance. Cross-country skiing has joined that list.

At this point we need to differentiate between *cardiovascular endurance* and *muscular endurance.*

Cardiovascular Endurance. Cardiovascular endurance refers to the ability of the heart and lungs to supply the body with oxygen and the body's subsequent ability to utilize the oxygen supplied (oxygen uptake). Most experts agree that training for cardiovascular endurance should consist of bouts of exercise that maintain the heart rate at 70-80 percent of maximum (i.e., approximately 180-200 beats per minute for men between ages 18-30) for a period of at least 25-30 minutes.

Cardiovascular endurance is a limiting factor in skiers' performance and should be trained for in the traditional manner, which we will explain later. But many athletes with finely trained cardiovascular systems will probably not ski very well simply because their muscles are not trained to do so. Training only for strength will not help the skating skier much, either. The new part of endurance training is directed at *muscular* endurance.

Muscular Endurance. Muscular endurance is the
ability of muscles to perform repeated contractions
over a long period of time. This type of endurance is
limited not only by the muscles' ability to utilize the
oxygen supplied by the cardiovascular system but also
by its ability to continue working in the presence of
lactic acid. In fact, the muscles under stress may well
become fatigued even before the cardiorespiratory system has exhausted its ability to furnish oxygen. Muscular endurance is developed by fairly long bouts of
muscle activity against resistance. For instance, whenever a weight-lifting exercise is performed for more
than 15-20 repetitions, the primary benefit is greater
endurance, with increased strength as the secondary
benefit. It is this combination of developing both
strength *and* endurance through exercise that has
been classified as training for muscular endurance.

Skating is more taxing on muscles than conventional styles of skiing, and therefore the programs in
this book will emphasize a gradual change from overdistance and ultraendurance training early in the
dryland season (May-June) to shorter, more specific
muscle activities later in the season before getting on
the snow and extending into the on-snow season.

We will describe this training agenda in greater
depth in chapter 9. For now, suffice it to say that you
can train for endurance with almost any kind of ski
training, dryland or on-snow, and that during the
course of a training year these bouts of exercise will
become more specific, more intense, and of shorter
duration. In other words, the training program will
focus more on muscular endurance as the season
progresses (see Figure 5.2).

Some examples of endurance training include the
following:

- *Running.* Steady pace, 30-90 minutes.
- *Biking.* 1-4 hours (20-90 miles) over flat or rolling
  terrain.
- *Slideboard.* 1 x 30 minutes, or 2 x 10-15 minutes,
  even pace.
- *Endurance weight lifting.* See chapter 8 on weight
  training.

Figure 5.2 Running is still one of the best ways to build endurance during the dryland season.

Anaerobic Threshold.   Anaerobic threshold (which you may see abbreviated to AT) refers to a certain point during strenuous activity when your body can no longer produce energy aerobically (i.e., in the presence of oxygen) and begins producing energy anaerobically (i.e., in the absence of oxygen). The by-product of anaerobic activity is lactic acid. Anaerobic threshold is just a fancy term for that point when you really start hurting. Experts have recently determined that endurance athletes, such as skiers, achieve the best advances in fitness when they perform most of their

endurance training at a level just below the point
where lactic acid is produced, that is, just below their
anaerobic threshold.

Very experienced athletes can recognize their own
anaerobic threshold by that slightly perceptible feeling
that tells them they are about to go under. Unfortunately, the way they learn to recognize that sinking
sensation accurately, and differentiate it from the regular ups and downs common to all exercise, is to have
hit the wall a few dozen times before. To avoid this
trial-and-error approach to training, a good formula
has been developed to help you find your individual
anaerobic threshold (which will differ from that of
other athletes).

To determine your anaerobic threshold you will
need a stopwatch and a friend to operate it, a pulse
monitor, and access to a 400-meter running track.
Mark off a 40-meter segment on each side of the track
(or on one side of a 200-meter track). This is a running
test, and a sufficient warm-up should be done before
the test begins. The runner will be performing eight
laps on the 400-meter track. The runner should start
out very slow and increase the speed slightly every
200 meters. Each 40-meter segment should be timed
and recorded. The runner should call out his or her
pulse at the end of every 40-meter timed segment.

The timer should record the results in a manner
similar to that seen in Table 1. You will notice a point
where the pulse rate continues to rise, but the times
for the 40-meter segments begin to get progressively
slower. This point is your anaerobic threshold. When
you reached that point in the test, your body began
producing lactic acid and your performance was nega-
tively affected.

The athlete in this test had an approximate anaerobic threshold of 185 beats per minute. This is a bit
high for many people, but each individual is different.
Maximum heart rate should not increase during the
duration of the ski season, but anaerobic threshold will
improve with training. You will be able to perform consistently at higher heart rates without producing lactic
acid.

With these results, you can regulate your effort
throughout a workout by means of a pulse-monitoring

Table 1 Example Test Results to Identify Anaerobic Threshold

Sample	Heart Rate	Time
1	130	14:00
2	138	13:10
3	150	11:86
4	156	11:10
5	163	10:30
6	170	9:96
7	179	9:50
8	184	8:60
9	185	8:50
10	183	8:60
11	185	8:70
12	189	9:00
13	190	9:40
14	194	9:90
15	190	10:00
16	185	10:93

device or stopwatch in order to maintain your level of effort near your anaerobic threshold and, theoretically, attain maximum benefit from your workout. Keep in mind that you should not expect very accurate results from the first test. Best results will be obtained after the athlete is more familiar with the nature of the test and the regular increases in intensity.

Do You Need a Pulse Monitor? A pulse monitor can be useful if you believe in the formulas and intend to train by them, but using one is not absolutely necessary. You will soon develop a feel for what you are doing, and you may prefer to train unburdened by computer technology strapped to your body. A plain old stopwatch or wristwatch can work just as well, once you have learned how to use it without interrupting the intensity of your workout. The easiest way to estimate your present heart rate is to count how many times your heart beats in a 6-second period and multiply by 10. Twelve beats in 6 seconds is an approximate pulse rate of 120 beats per minute.

Explained simply, the theory of anaerobic threshold training is that workouts will be more beneficial if you train at such a level that you do not wear out at the beginning of a workout. Keep the level of intensity consistent and at a level where you can finish as strongly as you began. This is also the way the most successful skiers race in competition.

Many skiers mistakenly believe that in doing workouts around AT guidelines one should never go over the "target pulse rate" during the workout. This idea is especially detrimental on skis because skiing involves uphills, downhills, and many changes of pace. A skier who tries to keep the pulse under 160 beats per minute on a steep uphill will be moving so slowly that he will increase the amount of static muscle activity in the legs and thus produce lactic acid, which is what the system was designed to avoid. We suggest that you view the target pulse as an average rate and not worry whether you go above or below it from time to time.

The basic thing to remember about endurance training is to start the training year with it and build all of your other workouts out of this endurance base. Endurance is the foundation, and no skier succeeds without it.

Interval Training

We like to classify interval training as endurance training with a twist. Intervals are a systematic type of workout that are usually done on a stopwatch or on a measured track or trail so that one can follow predetermined intervals of work and rest. For example, one of our favorite interval workouts, whether skiing, biking, or running, consists of one or two sets of six to ten repetitions of 60-second work periods in which each work period is followed by a 60-second rest. This is a common interval pattern called "minute on, minute off" and would be written as "10 x 60 on/60 off."

The object of interval training is to accustom your body to recovering more quickly from increases in effort. The end result will be to regularly raise your AT, which will enable you to work more consistently at a higher rate of energy output without producing lactic acid. Your body gets used to going faster, and as you grow stronger you can maintain that level of speed for longer intervals.

Most workouts involve intervals of one kind or another. The work/rest intervals can be long or short, depending on the specific workout and the time of year. They are generally longer in the summer and become shorter and more intense as the season progresses.

In addition to long and short intervals, there is another type of interval that we like to call *natural intervals*. Natural intervals occur when you ski a course or take a hilly run or bike ride. There is an increased work interval as you press up the hills and a recovery interval on the downhills. In this way almost all of

Figure 5.3 Interval tours are a great way to get out on the ski trails during the summer and fall. Low walk the uphills and jog the flats and downhills.

your skiing will be an interval session, as will all of your racing.

The faster you can recover, the faster your average rate of speed will be. If there's ever a question as to which type of workout to do on a given day, do intervals (see Figure 5.3).

Some examples of interval training include the following:

* *Running.* 2-3 x (5 x 300-meter run/100-meter walk).
* *Bike.* 3 minutes on/3 off, 2 on/2 off, 1 on/1 off, 30 seconds on/30 seconds off, 1 minute on/1 minute off, 2 minutes on/2 minutes off, 3 minutes on/ 3 minutes off.
* *Hill loops.* 6-10 x 20-40 seconds hill run, 45-90 seconds jog down. Repeating.
* *Interval tour.* Best done on hiking or skiing trails jogging the flats and downhills, low walking or sidestepping the uphills at a harder pace for a total of 15-90 minutes.

There are many other types of interval workouts, but rather than list them all here we will list them as examples in chapter 10 in our discussion on setting up training programs. Do interval workouts when you can't think of what else to do and appreciate them as the highest quality workout you can do in your training program.

Tempo Training

Tempo training differs from interval training in that there is no preset measure of the recovery period. Instead, in tempo training you take a "full rest" between work periods. The work is performed at what we will call *race pace*, that is, with practically an all-out effort. Whereas endurance training and intervals are aerobic workouts, tempos will often push athletes into an anaerobic state. Tempos teach you how to race by allowing you to experiment with your body's limits at racing speed while avoiding the damaging effects of a full-length race.

Tempos are most effectively used in less technical workouts such as biking and running. Doing tempos on roller skis does you no good because the degree of

effort required and the amount of lactic acid produced
will destroy your technique on every set. All this will
get you is a lot of bad technical habits that will be
hard to break when you finally get onto your skis. Use
tempo training when you are free to concentrate on
the quality of the effort and leave more technical workouts for another time (see Figure 5.4).

Most tempo training will also involve somewhat
longer work periods than intervals, but keep in mind
that you get a full rest after each tempo and that the
workout will stop when the last run was significantly
more difficult than the first. A full rest should never require more than 8-10 minutes. If it does, it's time to go
home. Never train to exhaustion. You should always
have one step left at the end of a workout.

Tempos are one of the most taxing—and poten-
tially damaging—types of workouts and require lots of
rest after the workout is completed. Thus they should
never constitute more than 12-15 percent of your
weekly schedule and should not be included in your
training schedule until you have 2-3 months of base

Figure 5.4 A bicycle is the best tool for tempo workouts. Bike workouts yield both muscular and cardiovascular benefits, and biking uti-
lizes the same lower body muscles that are used in skating.

training. Many young skiers become addicted to tempo training, probably because this type of workout makes them feel like they are working extra hard. But doing too many tempos in your program spells overtraining, even for the most superbly conditioned athletes. Temper your desire for hard work with a little common sense, and tempos will remain an important and beneficial part of your training schedule (see Figure 5.5).

The following are examples of tempo training:

- *Biking.* 5 x 6 minutes, on the flat, with full rests between each.
- *Running.* 5, 3, 2, 1, 2, 3, 5 minutes tempo run, full rest between each (walk or jog).
- *Hill tempos.* 6-12 x full-effort uphill runs, low walking, bounding, or running backwards; full rest while walking down (this is the toughest of the tempo workouts).

Figure 5.5 Hill tempo running is one of the most intense forms of dryland training.

Speed/Sprint Training

Speed or sprint training will be new to many skiers. Now that speed is such a crucial part of competitive skiing, good racers need a certain amount of snap in their strokes. This type of leg speed can only be developed by doing workouts or exercises that make your legs and arms move faster than they will when you are on skis. Sprint and speed workouts will also be anaerobic and will produce lactic acid like tempos do. Thus it seems logical that sprint/speed workouts should be concentrated in nontechnical work sessions. Biking is especially well suited for speed work because it lends itself to the highest rate of leg revolutions per minute.

Power Versus Speed. The emphasis in speed training should be divided between sprints for explosive power (such as uphill sprints or leaping exercises) and sprints for leg speed (such as seated bike sprints or downhill runs). The combination of power and speed is what will develop an explosive skating stroke, so don't train to develop one facet at the expense of the other.

Sprint workouts are relatively enjoyable and don't take much time, so we usually like to schedule them at a time when we might be tempted to shorten or skip a longer workout, such as late Friday afternoon. Doing sprints with a partner or a group is very beneficial and much more fun. You must remember, however, that skiers don't really need much speed work before September. Even at the peak of the season sprints should never constitute more than 6-10 percent of your training in any given week (see Figure 5.6).

Some examples of sprint training are the following:

- *Bike sprints (for power).* 10 x 20-30 seconds uphill sprint (standing).
- *Bike sprints (for leg speed).* 2 x (10 x 20 seconds) high pedal rpm (seated).
- *Sprint runs.* 3 x 60 meter build-up run, 3 x 80 meter build-up run, 3 x 50 meter low walk build, 3 x 30 meter low walk sprint, 3 x 50 meter sprint run, 3 x 100 meter sprint run, 3 x 10 right leg and 10 left leg hops uphill, 3 x 12-20 broad jumps uphill, 3 x 10 seconds run uphill, 3 x 12 broad jumps, 3 x 50 meter low walk leaps, 3 x 60 meter build-up run.

Figure 5.6   Uphill sprints of 10-30 seconds are a very effective means of building power.

Strength Training

Training for strength is usually thought of as working with weights. Skiers don't need as much strength training as speed skaters need because their body position is not as low and their races are not so short and explosive. Nevertheless, developing a good, low cross-country skating position requires considerable strength, especially in the back, hips, and thighs. During the first race of the season is no time to discover that you don't have enough strength. Strength training will be discussed in detail in chapter 8, which deals exclusively with weight training.

Technical Training

Some training sessions in our program concentrate solely on the development of technique. In this category we include some slideboard and roller ski workouts, one on-snow session a week during the winter, and almost all roller skate workouts. These are minimum-effort workouts, based on the principle of exaggeration discussed in chapter 7.

Skiers can learn some very damaging technical habits during the dryland season by trying to push too hard during "specific" workouts. Specificity is fine, but only if technique is not lost in the effort to "get a good workout." There is a time to push hard and a time to concentrate on technical refinement. The time to put the two together does not come until late in the dryland season and when you are actually on the snow.

Many skiers may resist this idea and may claim that we are arguing against the specificity in training that has been the core of skiing programs for the last decade. In a way, we are. We have seen many skiers at all levels train the entire summer on roller skis or, worse, on roller skates, thinking that this is just like skiing. They all ended up ruined. No single apparatus or exercise is good enough to act as a replacement for skiing in the summer. With dryland training all you can do is imitate and exaggerate the technical motions of skiing and increase your body's memory of them. You cannot do this effectively during a roller workout in which you are also trying to keep your pulse high enough to get a good aerobic workout.

The workouts that are classified as "technical" are designed to be done at a low level of effort in order to allow you to concentrate on exaggerating the technical fine points. Roller skates can be beneficial for technical training but should not be used as a tool for endurance or interval workouts.

The following workouts are examples of technical training:

- *Roller skating.* 20 x 30 seconds, easy and technically correct, exaggerating knee bend, body position, and heel snap.
- *Roller skiing.* 10 x 5 minutes, low effort, perfect technique, making every stroke a mirror image of the last. Done on flat terrain, coasting 3-5 minutes between each technical set.

This type of "technical interval" is very common in our programs. The work period is performed at low effort, with emphasis on exaggerated technique, whereas the rest period is to ensure that fatigue does not impair your technical practice, as well as to allow time for coaching or feedback. Slow, exaggerated technical work can build lactic acid from static muscle activity, so the rest periods will be welcome by the end of the workout. These technical sessions are not the cinch they may appear to be.

Recreation/Coordination Training

This last category is included to keep your training from becoming too stale or serious. Your training will be more beneficial if you can enjoy it more, and including a couple of workouts a week, whose sole purpose is physical recreation is one way to keep yourself fresh.

Included in this category are hiking, soccer, basketball, ultimate Frisbee, touch football, aerobic dance, water skiing, and many other popular sports. These types of training diversions will allow you a chance to overcome boredom but still receive the benefits of a workout. The coordination and competitiveness required in games such as these will only enhance your athletic development. You should take advantage of the opportunity to enjoy your training by forgetting about being a skier now and then. Both mind and body need the chance to play from time to time, so don't be afraid to let it happen.

Every workout mentioned in the remainder of this book fits into one of these seven categories. The correct way to organize them and develop a training program that emphasizes each type of workout at the proper time will be covered in chapter 9.

What About Everything Else? This book is designed to serve the needs of the intermediate to advanced skier. We are assuming that the readers are familiar with the elements of training for conventional skiing. Thus we have chosen not to spend time on topics which have not changed since the advent of skating techniques. Primary among these topics are stretching, warm-up, and warm-down. It is expected that all athletes will follow a flexibility program and incorporate a complete warm-up and warm-down into every workout.

There are other questions this book chooses not to address that should be dealt with the same as for conventional skiing. These include general health, diet, vitamin supplements, drug consumption, travel for competition, altitude training, and competitive habits. This book deals with skating only. Elements of skiing and ski training that have not changed for the skating skier will not be covered. In the interest of brevity topics such as the ones just mentioned are left to other sources.

Dryland Training Principles and Simulation Exercises

6

Swimmers can swim all year, and runners can run in every season. But in order to ski a skier must find some snow. And unless you have the cash to keep yourself in perpetual winter by chasing the snow all over the globe, then you will eventually have to do some dryland training.

Many skiers actually learn to enjoy this off-season training regimen, and more than one good racer has admitted that the joy of being a skier comes more from the training than from racing or winning. In any case, considering how little time a skier spends actually competing, taking pleasure in your training lifestyle rather than basing your level of satisfaction on race results is probably a healthy attitude. If you can't enjoy your training, then don't expect great racing results.

In this chapter, we will introduce you to the principles of dryland training and how they relate to specific exercises, as well as a few tricks of the trade to make your life as an off-season skier more pleasant. Ideas for training nontechnically with running and biking and the like have already been discussed, and both weight training and highly specific workouts will be covered in following chapters. That leaves this chapter to discuss the simulation exercises for training skiing muscles and some general guidelines to utilize in all dryland activities.

Your Training Closet

Before we even get started, there are one or two things you can do to make yourself more comfortable for dryland training and simulation exercises. First, get yourself an inexpensive but sturdy pair of running or training shoes. Much of the dryland training you'll be doing will eat shoes alive, regardless of their design or price tag, so get a pair that you can afford to abuse. We have always had most success with certain training shoes that have good lateral support and waffle soles, such as those designed for trail running, but we have used everything from soccer cleats to basketball hightops, so let personal preference be your guide.

Second, find some durable, loose-fitting training shorts and some expendable T-shirts. Then prepare yourself for some weird laundry problems! Dryland

Figure 6.1   Typical dryland training clothes.

athletes kick up a lot of dirt and spend a lot of time rolling around on the ground or juggling dirty sandbag weights, especially during circuit training. Later in the season polypropylene underwear and outer layers of clothing will come in handy, but keep in mind that training doesn't have to be a fashion show. All we can recommend is to have a few changes of training clothes, or you risk losing your training partners! (See Figure 6.1.)

Simulation Exercises

You can't actually learn ski technique in the dryland season, but you can accustom the specific muscles involved in skiing to performing the motions involved in skiing. The way to do this is through specific, technical workouts (as described in chapter 5) and simulation exercises that replicate the skills and movements utilized in on-snow skiing.

These exercises can be used for endurance, interval, strength, and even tempo training, but in all the emphasis will be on technique and correctness of form. Simulation exercises will accustom the skier to the vital practice of designating the development of some element of technique as a goal in every workout. We'll discuss this idea of technical concentration after describing the exercises themselves.

A wordy description of each exercise would be quite tedious, so we'll let illustrations do most of the talking and use this next section for extra information for each exercise. Any of the following exercises can be used individually, as the basic activity for an entire workout, or as a station in a circuit.

- *Dry skating.* Lateral skating steps, alternating legs performed 1-10 minutes with or without weights. The push is made with the heel. Suggested tempo 30-50 per minute (see Figure 6.2).
- *Double hops.* An explosive form of dry skating involving a lateral leap with a small hop on the landing foot before leaping back again. The push is made with the heel. Suggested tempo 25-45 per minute.

Figure 6.2 Dry skating, lateral skating steps. Make skating motions from side to side, never moving forward. Note full foot contact at all stages of the push. Use either single-stick or double-stick arm motion.

- *Side steps.* Lateral steps (as in dry skating) taken in one direction only (moving sideways). Side steps can be done as hill climbs or on the level. The push is made with the heel. Suggested tempo 40-65 per minute (see Figure 6.3).
- *Gunther hops.* We don't know who "Gunther" was, but we have always called these "Gunther hops" and see no reason to change. This is called a *leg switch* exercise. Jump in place off of one leg at a time, extending the free leg to the side. Try to

Figure 6.3 Side steps, front view.

Figure 6.4 Gunther hops. The free leg is directed to the side, never falling to the rear. Try to keep the hop as a midfoot push.

make the push with the heel as much as possible. Gunther hops can be done with or without weights. Suggested tempo 45-65 per minute (see Figure 6.4).

- *Forward leg switch.* Like a Gunther hop, but the free leg extends back or under the body with each jump. Forward leg switches can be done with or without weights. Suggested tempo 45-65 per minute (see Figure 6.5).

- *Low walk.* Also called a *duck walk*, this exercise is performed just like its name implies: walking in a low, bent-over position with deeply bent knees. Each stride will be 4-6 feet long, and the toes of your recovering foot will drag along the ground with each step. That's a good reason to do this exercise only on grass. Arms can be swung freely, as in walking, or held behind the back for relaxation. Low walking is generally done without weights, for

Figure 6.5   Forward leg switch.

Figure 6.6   Low walk. Make long strides, extending the pushing leg fully on each step. Swing arms freely just like walking. Drag your toes if it helps you keep your balance.

periods of 1-60 minutes, constantly or as an interval tour. The pushing is done with the toes as in running or walking. Suggested tempo 60-120 steps per minute (see Figure 6.6).

- *Low walk leaps.* Also called *bounding* when done with poles in a more upright position, low walk leaps are explosive leaps performed on the flat or an uphill. As in low walking, the pushing is done with the toes. These are exercises for developing strength and muscular endurance, not necessarily technique. Suggested tempo 50-85 per minute.
- *High steps.* These are a type of low walk performed with a high, knee-to-chest stepping motion. Use a very slow tempo, concentrating on extension, relaxation, and balance (see Figure 6.7).

Figure 6.7 High steps.

- *Broad jumps.* These are continuous standing broad jumps just like the "frog jumps" you used to do in grammar school gym class. Broad jumps are the most explosive exercise, on flats or uphills, and are a major part of sprint/power workouts. Do 5-30 jumps in a row. Suggested tempo 40-60 per minute (see Figure 6.8).
- *One-leg hops.* These are continuous broad jumps performed on one leg, 5-30 in a row. They are very explosive and are a part of sprint/power workouts (see Figure 6.9).
- *In-and-out jumps.* These are like a "jumping jack" leg motion but are done from deeply bent knees. These jumps are excellent for building up the hips and upper thighs. Suggested tempo 50-75 per minute (see Figure 6.10).
- *Step overs.* Step overs involve falling from one side to the other, across the standing leg. This is a good

Figure 6.8   Broad jumps.

Figure 6.9   One-leg hops.

Figure 6.10 In-and-out jumps.

exercise for developing balance and body control. Use a slow relaxed tempo (see Figure 6.11).

All of these exercises are specific to skiing in that they work the same muscle groups that are used in skating. Learning to do these exercises properly and including them as a part of your workout programs will make you a better skier next winter.

Dryland Basics

The following guidelines relate to all dryland training. These are the basic principles to remember during any dryland workout.

1. Keep your hips and shoulders square while performing all exercises, as well as in all other phases of ski training.
2. Maintain a quiet upper body; that is, maintain relaxed positioning and avoid thrashing of the arms, head, or shoulders. Practice running, biking, and all other dryland exercises with your elbows held close to your sides.
3. Keep your feet oriented parallel to one another or even slightly pigeon-toed during all exercises. This

Figure 6.11 Step overs.

will emphasize the heel push and imitate the binding orientation on the ski.

4. The deeper the knee bend at which exercises can be performed, the more beneficial they will be. Ninety degrees is the ideal to strive for, but going below 90 degrees is risking knee injury.

5. In all lateral and leg switch exercises, the emphasis should remain on keeping your weight over the rear half of the foot and pushing with a strong snap of the heel (see Figure 6.12).

6. You do not necessarily need to emphasize arms and legs together in an exercise, like skiers who used to rig up stretch bands to pull on while they were on the slideboard (a particularly absurd practice that produced countless bad habits). Unless you have poles in your hands, we recommend a relaxed, diagonal type of arm swing (as in walking) or keeping your hands behind your back like a speed skater. This is good practice for balance and relaxation. If you can keep your upper body quiet while your hands are kept behind your back, then you'll have no trouble doing it when your

Figure 6.12 Side steps, side view. Notice how the push is directed straight to the side. The entire foot maintains contact with the ground through the end of the stroke.

hands are free. Many of these exercises work the same muscles that are used in skating but do not lend themselves to being performed with poles. In dry skating, for example, all the movement is lateral; no forward movement is involved. Dry skating is like skating in place. You can't use your poles very easily if your body cannot move forward with each pole stroke.

7. When you do swing your arms, swing them straight forward and back, not across the midline of the body. This will help you to maintain proper alignment and prevent the body from twisting.

8. Keep your head up. You will need to be looking and thinking ahead when you get on the snow next winter, so don't get in the habit of doing these exercises with your head down.

What to do. By now you must be wondering exactly what to do with all these goofy hops and jumps. You can use the following sample workouts to incorporate dryland exercises into your program. Many more will be illustrated in chapter 9 on setting up programs.

- *Endurance low walk.* 5-45 minutes straight low walking on the flat.
- *Interval tour.* 20-90 minutes of jogging flats and downhills, low walking all uphills. Interval tours provide a great excuse to summer train on the ski trails.
- *Endurance run/dry skate.* This is a continuous motion workout in which you perform exercises for a set time and intersperse each set with running/jogging at an easy pace for about 5 minutes. We suggest a schedule similar to 5, 3, 2, 10, 2, 3, 5 minutes of dry skating or a combination of other dryland exercises, with a 5-minute rest jog after each work set. Try changing exercises every minute.
- *Power sprints.* 3 x 60-meter sprint run, 3 x 60-meter low walk buildup, 3 x 40-meter leaps, 3 x 10 broad jumps uphill, 3 x 10 right/10 left one-leg hops uphill, 3 x 20 broad jumps on the flat, 3 x 60-meter sprint run.
- *Circuit.* The circuit combines general fitness exercises (push-ups, sit-ups, etc.) with specific dryland

exercises in a circuit with 10-14 stations. All exercises can be performed with or without a weight. This particular workout will be explained more thoroughly in chapter 8.

• *Hill loops.* Run uphill 30-45 seconds, jog 30 seconds, dry skate (or do some other simulation exercise) 60 seconds, jog 30 seconds, low walk 60 seconds, leap 20 seconds, and jog to bottom of hill to begin next lap.

The ways of combining dryland exercises will be limited only by your imagination. We may tend to emphasize leg workouts at the expense of the arms. Frankly, most of the power in skating should be coming from the legs, and the role of the arms is even more specialized in skating than in conventional skiing. The faster the rate of travel, the less important the role of poling becomes. In the interest of completeness, arm work will be covered in detail in chapter 8.

Injuries.   Exaggerated technique means deep knee bend and low body position. Skating skiers will have to be more careful of their backs and knees. If you train correctly, you need not fear injury from skating. Many injuries in the last few years have been blamed on skating and the demands it places on the joints, especially the knees. The main reason for all those injuries was that skiers did not prepare those stress areas during the dryland season. Very few world-class speed skaters suffer from knee or lower back injuries, and their sport requires more extreme stresses on the skating muscles and corresponding joints.

The way to avoid injury is to begin the dryland season easily, working gradually into the deeper knee bend. Pay attention to any warning signals from your back and knees and ease off if you feel any joint pain. Spend the dryland season acclimatizing your body to the particular stresses of skating, and you will not end up wasting the ski season with skating injuries that could have been prevented with careful preseason training.

Roller Skis, Roller Skates, and Slideboard

7

Few of us have the financial freedom to spend the entire summer in the southern hemisphere in pursuit of year-round snow. But if you are trapped in a warm summer climate you might as well make the best of it. The way for skiers to do this is to perform some exercises that closely simulate the motions and stresses of actual skiing. These types of workouts are termed *ultraspecific* and include training on roller skis, roller blades, and slideboards.

None of these training activities provides a perfect workout, and none can even come close to replacing skiing. In many ways, however, these activities are as close to actual skiing as we can come, and we will have to make the best of them. The most important thing to remember about any summer training, especially what we will call "specificity training," is that you cannot learn to skate in the summertime—not on roller skis, not on roller blades, not on ice skates. The best you can do during the summer is to prepare the skating muscles and systems for the types of stress they are likely to be subjected to during actual skiing, without developing any nasty "dryland habits." This is done by relying on an old speed skater's trick called *exaggeration*.

Exaggeration

Exaggeration is the key to all technical workouts. Only by exaggerating the correct technical form during the dryland season can you avoid the bad habits that can develop as a result of specificity exercises that are imperfect substitutes for skiing.

Always remember that nothing you can do in the summer is anywhere nearly as difficult as skiing itself. Many of the more specific exercises will feel like skiing and may convince you that your skill on skis will be just like that on roller skis. This is not the case, so don't be fooled. Many anxious and ambitious skiers are greatly disappointed during the ski season when they realize that being the "dryland world champion" is no guarantee that they will perform well during the actual ski season. The best that summer training can do is to prepare you for the ski season physically by training the skating muscles. It cannot teach you *how* to ski.

Exaggeration forces you to constantly concentrate on the technical essentials of each stroke. Humans don't learn best by merely seeing something done the proper way. If you want to get someone's attention or have them remember something clearly, it is best to exaggerate what you are trying to teach. This is how you must deal with yourself in technical workouts. You are divided into two halves: the teacher and the student. In order for your body to learn the correct skating motions, your brain must instruct it to exaggerate its movements in training (see Figure 7.1).

This is how your dryland training relates to skiing. If you want to ski with an average knee bend of 105 degrees, then you should spend the summer training with a bend of about 95 degrees. Due to the greater balance and tension factors involved in skiing, on skis your average knee bend will increase 5-10 degrees. Thus if you thought that your summer training would carry over technically onto the snow, and you spent your summer training at a knee bend of 105 degrees, you would spend the winter skiing practically straight-legged. This is only one example of how dryland training technique must be modifiied to replicate the demands of actual skiing.

Roller Skiing

When all skiing was diagonal stride and double-poling, roller skis emerged as an effective means of

Figure 7.1   Roller skating allows exaggeration of ideal ski skating technique. Notice how all four wheels left the surface simultaneously at the end of the stroke.

training specifically. We are not saying they were the perfect training tool. Many skiers got a little carried away with the whole idea, but roller skis were and still are the most effective way to create the "feel" of skiing during the off season. The only problem for us is that roller skis are no longer as effective for the skating skier as they were for the diagonal strider.

Although roller skis are not the miracle training tool people once thought they were, you should still keep a place for them in your training program. They can be used quite effectively in technical exaggeration sessions and in moderate endurance or interval workouts. The drawbacks of training on roller skis must be intelligently risked to enable you to keep some of the "feel" of actual skiing in your training program.

Let's look at the advantages and disadvantages of training on roller skis so that we can fit roller ski workouts into our overall program.

Disadvantages.

1. The type of roller ski that most of us can afford to own is much heavier and harder to maneuver than a normal pair of skis. This causes skiers to develop many small technical quirks to compensate for the added weight. As a result, skiers who trained all summer on roller skis often pick their feet up too high and experience difficulty in maintaining proper stroke tempo.
2. The fact that you train on a paved surface on roller skis affects the way you plant your poles. Skiers who do nothing but roller ski often plant their poles rather tentatively. Balance problems and the fear of falling associated with roller skis also cause most skiers to plant their poles farther out from the edge of the ski. Both of these undesirable habits are easily acquired by training on roller skis and carry over into your ski technique.
3. The width of the roller ski prevents you from ever bringing your feet completely together, a habit that will be disastrous when you get on the snow.
4. Roller skiing presents the obvious danger of injury from falls or losing battles with automobiles.
5. In many places roller skiing is restricted or even illegal.
6. Roller skiing equipment is expensive, and replacement parts are not always readily available.
7. Most roller skis (and roller skates) are faster than actual skiing and can thus cause hitches in your rhythm and poling habits.

Advantages.

1. First and foremost, roller skis will make you *feel* like a skier. This is a very important facet of your training attitude. If you cannot remember exactly why you are doing all this summer training, you may not always be motivated to get out and do it. Roller skis allow you to get out and ski. Even with all its faults, roller skiing is still as close as you can come to actual skiing in the off season.
2. Since the invention of two-wheeled roller skis that can actually "edge" like a ski, roller skis are becoming a better means of accurate simulation for skating skiers.
3. Except for spills, very few serious injuries are associated with the use of roller skis. Pay attention to your elbows and knees for minor stresses from excessive road-shock vibration.
4. Knowing the disadvantages of roller skiing can help you to avoid problems by encouraging you to exaggerate correct technique in your specific training. In this way, specific methods of training can serve to preserve or improve your skiing skills for next winter.

What's New? We are assuming that you have had some experience with roller skiing in the past, and rather than waste your time instructing you in their use, this section will be used to discuss how the use of roller skis should be changing with the shift of emphasis from conventional ski techniques to skating.

The primary change skiers should make in their programs in using roller skis is to decrease the amount of time spent on them for distance workouts. This distance time can be replaced by quality training time, such as technique work or intervals on the roller skis, but all this "just skiing" that people have been doing is bound to be technically harmful and does very little to help you to build more quality into your schedule.

Do most of your overdistance and endurance work on a less technical apparatus, such as a bicycle, rowing machine, or slideboard. This will help you to avoid fatigue-induced technical problems that may result from trying too often to develop fitness and technique in the same workout. Early in the dryland season, you will have very little need to train as specifically as roller skiing anyway. Later as you approach the skiing season, however, much more work will be done on the technically specific tools such as skates, skis, and slideboards. This is the time you will want your skating muscles to be trained for, so spend the bulk of the summer training the muscles and systems and leave something as technical as roller skiing for later. Begin roller skiing workouts in late July or early August and increase the distance and quality of your training as you near the on-snow season.

Care and Feeding of Roller Skis.   Roads are not commonly known for their cleanliness, so you should check your roller skis regularly for wear or need of maintenance. If they are not sealed, clean out the bearings once in a while (sand in the bearings will stop a ski faster than glue). You would also be wise to tighten up the axle nuts from time to time. Roller skis are surprisingly limited by the sudden absence of a wheel, and a downhill at 40 miles per hour in rush-hour traffic is no time to discover this for yourself!

People have also been altering their two-wheeled roller skis by shortening them. This is easy enough to do and does seem to make the skis lighter, less cumbersome, and a little closer to actual skating on skis. Our suggestion is to remove the front wheel assembly and saw off 6 to 10 inches. Cut any more than that and you are making it back into a roller skate. Manufacturers are now producing shorter roller skis for skaters, but, frankly, some of them are too short. Make your decision based on your own comfort. Our only recommendation is not to use skis that are too short. Why volunteer to inherit the disadvantages of roller skates?

Roller Skating

What has already been said about roller skiing goes double for roller skates (or "roller blades" as they are commonly called). Because they are shorter, easier, and more maneuverable than roller skis, roller skates are especially dangerous as technical tools for skiers. We have observed skiers on roller skates developing unbelievably sloppy habits. The way to avoid this is to leave longer technical workouts to the roller skis and slideboards and utilize roller skates for what they are best suited: exaggeration.

Never use roller skates for a tour or any distance or endurance work. Until you become absolutely efficient on them technically, we do not even recommend doing any intervals on roller skates other than technique intervals. Roller skates work for the type of technical exaggeration that your body will remember, and in this way they provide a great tool for augmenting your summer training on roller skis. But they will never be a replacement for roller skis, and you should not think of substituting one for the other.

Roller skates can be very helpful in learning the tempo and rhythm of skating strokes because they are more maneuverable and forgiving than roller skis. Extra care should be taken every time you use them, however, because they can be the source of numerous bad habits.

Equipment. If you choose to train on roller skates, our primary recommendation is to avoid the plastic hockey-style boots that are usually sold with the roller blade assembly. That amount of ankle support is both unnecessary and totally unlike skiing and will cause you to develop some habits about ski/blade orientation during the push that simply will not transfer onto the snow. Shorter, more flexible boots for roller blades are now being made, and these are probably worth some investigation. If you can find them, try lighter, leather boots similar to speed skater's boots. You don't need to be afraid of this because ankle strength is not a major factor in skating. Remember that the push in skating goes down into the snow, not out across it. As a result, all the pushing goes straight down through the sole of the shoe, and therefore any "ankle drooping" is a balance/confidence problem, not an ankle problem. If you do choose to use the plastic boots, try to keep the top laces a little looser and don't depend so much on the boot for support (see Figure 7.2).

Figure 7.2   Roller skates for practicing cross-country skating technique.

Care and Feeding of Roller Skates.   As with roller skis, the best thing you can do for roller skates is to keep the bearings clean and rotate the wheels on a regular basis to keep them from wearing away on the inside edge only. Save those old, worn-out wheels. They work great for building your own roller boards for arm workouts (see chapter 8).

Slideboard

Finally we get to a technical apparatus that you can really pound on. Slideboards are more forgiving of technical error than roller skates and roller skis and are less likely to produce gross errors in your actual skiing. Slideboarding is just close enough to skiing to provide a good, specific workout but still far enough removed from skiing to allow you to do extended, quality workouts without ruining what skiing technique you have already developed.

Building Your Own Slideboard.   A number of companies are producing slideboards, but we haven't seen a good one yet. Building a slideboard is such an easy job that you may as well do it yourself (see Figure 7.3).

front

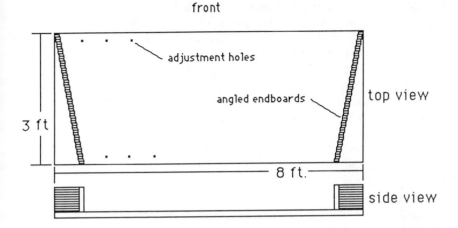

Figure 7.3 Slideboard elevation.

The easiest way to build your own slideboard is to buy a 4 x 8 foot (1.25 x 2.4 meter) piece of high-grade plywood and a 4 x 8 foot (1.25 x 2.4 meter) piece of smoothest (glasslike) formica or linoleum. Put these together with contact cement. Make endboards out of 2 x 4s (5 x 10 centimeter) or 4 x 4s (10 x 10 centimeter) and pad them with carpet scraps or worn-out sleeping bag pads. Remember two things about endboards: drilling extra holes (see Figure 7.3) will make one of the boards movable to shorten or lengthen the board, and angling the endboards to flare out to the front (a 6-inch difference) will make your push much more effective and reduce potential injuries to the feet and ankles.

You can ask a carpenter to put a piano hinge down the middle of your board to make it more portable, and sliding across the seam shouldn't bother you much. The board you see in the photos is a 10-foot (3-meter) board, shortened to 8 feet (2.4 meters). The slideboard shown is fairly plain, but customizing your board is limited only by your imagination.

Pointers. You can do certain things during slideboard workouts to ensure that you maintain correct technical standards. You can't really hurt your technique on a slideboard, but neglecting certain fine points will make your slideboard workouts less beneficial. Foremost in this respect is that you must always keep your shoulders, hips, and feet square in respect to the

imaginary "line of travel." Thus you will still be leading with the hips, not the shoulders, and your feet will
always point straight ahead, never duck-footed. The
best way to check your positioning is to set up your
board in front of a mirror and watch yourself for
mistakes.

Make certain that you keep pushing with the heel.
This can be made easier by angling the endboards
slightly (as shown in Figure 7.3) so that when you
stand facing forward with your pushing foot next to
the endboard, the entire outside of your foot and not
just the outside of the ball of the foot will be contact-
ing the endboard. A little padding really helps.
Nagging bruises or even bone spurs can keep you off
the board for a while, so spend the cash for a sleeping
bag pad you can cut up for making bumper pads.

What Length?   A slideboard that is somewhere between 2 to 2.5 meters long seems to work best for
most people. Speed skaters generally like to keep their
boards between 2.4 to 3 meters long, but they are
working from a lower knee bend and therefore produce
a longer stroke than a skier. It is easiest to use the
board at a shorter length when doing a long "down
time" because keeping the tempo high is easier when
you don't have to push so hard just to move across the
board. Lengthen the board for more explosive sessions,
such as intervals.

What Tempo?   In general, skiers overemphasize fast
tempo on the slideboard. It's better to let your tempo
happen naturally and lengthen the board or wear a
weight vest to make the workout more difficult.
Remember that slideboarding is still a technical workout, and the emphasis should be on *exaggerating* ski
technique, not re-creating it. Use a lower position than
normal and fully extend each stroke. Keep your tempo
on the slideboard within reason. Don't loaf between
strokes, but don't blast yourself off the board, either.
Relax and concentrate on getting maximum quality
out of each stroke; let the tempo happen on its own
(see Figure 7.4).

Figure 7.4 Slideboard technique. Low recovery with single-stick arm swing. The body position shown here is a bit lower than that used by most skiers. Notice how push occurs off the middle of a flat foot. Feet remain oriented straight ahead to the imagined direction of travel. The body should twist as little as possible and does not bob up and down.

Care and Feeding of Slideboards.   Here's a list of suggestions to keep your slideboard healthy and in prime condition:

1. Store the board on its edge to keep it free of dust.
2. Wear the cheapest rag wool socks available over your shoes. They protect your feet from injury, and the slight heel lift gained from wearing shoes is a limiting factor in what knee bend you can comfortably maintain.

3. Don't walk off of the board in those socks because they can pick up lots of dirt that can scratch the surface and slow down its action. Likewise, don't walk across the board unless you have the socks on over your shoes.

4. Your board will slide around least on a carpeted floor. We also suggest using sandbag weights, or robust friends and relatives, to help hold the ends of the board. It's rather unpleasant when the board goes one way and you go the other in midpush!

5. Treat the surface of the board with silicone spray or furniture polish before each use. Keep an old towel handy to wipe down the board before every use.

What About Your Arms?   You really can't do much for your arms during a slideboard workout other than learning to relax them so that they do not throw off the alignment of your upper body. All the motion is lateral, so you certainly cannot make any use of your poles. Mimic a double-poling motion or swing your arms in a diagonal fashion, but always straight forward and back, never across the midline of the body. It is never necessary, nor beneficial, to set up any kind of stretch bands or pulleys to yank on while you are on the slideboard. They will only throw you off balance, and you will end up pulling yourself around the board with your arms, which is not the point. Spend portions of longer work intervals with your hands behind your back like a speed skater for practice in balance and relaxation. It's not as easy as it sounds (see Figure 7.5).

The Latest Craze in Slideboards.   You may have seen pictures of slideboards with a hump in the middle for emphasizing the high recovery of the free leg in certain skating strokes (specifically SVS, where a low recovery is used). If you want to practice that (and you should), why not just stay down after hitting the endboard and recover the free leg by bringing the knee

Figure 7.5 Slideboard with standing recovery. The skier "stands up" after hitting the board at the end of each stroke using a double-pole arm swing. This technique emphasizes slower tempo and concentrates on the load-up phase of each stroke. Notice how feet remain parallel, body is oriented straight ahead, and the hips lead each stroke.

to the chest (exactly like on the snow)? This will also save you the trouble and expense of building another board.

These "hill slideboards" may sound like a good idea, but there are technical reasons to avoid them. The idea on a slideboard is to step out toward the middle of the board on each push, leading with the hip. Having that hill in the middle of an already short board makes you stutter this step and begin the push by leading with the free foot (reaching for the bump to keep from falling over it). This causes you to rotate the shoulders. A regular slideboard is tough enough to master without having another one around that will cause you to develop bad technical habits (see Figure 7.6).

That's about enough on the specific workout tools. More can be learned by studying the illustrations than

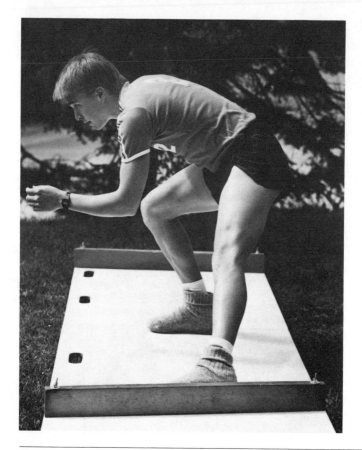

Figure 7.6 Slideboard technique, side view. Note feet pointed straight ahead and push directed straight to the side. Shoulders do not bob. They maintain a constant level orientation.

by reading our descriptions. Workouts for all three of these highly specific exercises will be listed in chapter 9, and the optimal times to emphasize specificity workouts will be discussed in chapter 10.

Weight Training and Strength Work

8

This chapter has a simple title but will cover much more than just lifting weights. Skating skiers will realize the growing need for strength and muscle endurance in their programs, and this chapter will give you some ideas and guidelines for incorporating strength work into your training schedule throughout both the dryland and skiing seasons.

Weight training for skiers can be divided into the following four workout types:

1. *Strength weights.* Most of us view strength work as regular weight lifting in the weight room. Many skiers should take more advantage of strength training because the amount of strength involved in skiing is always increasing, but it should not be the core of their weight-training program. Strength weights will be done with fairly heavy weights and high intensity in sets of no more than 10-12 repetitions. This may be done on weight machines or with free weights.
2. *Endurance weights.* You can train for endurance with weights by using moderate weight amounts and high repetitions (20-100 reps). This type of training is specifically designed to improve muscular endurance.
3. *Circuit training.* Circuit training might be called "interval weights." This involves doing exercises in a circuit with free weights, sandbags, or body weight. Circuit training builds strength and endurance but not to the degree as strength weights or endurance weights.

4. *Maintenance training.* You can't be traveling around to ski races hauling a thousand pounds of barbells and sandbags along with you. Maintenance training is a series of exercises utilizing body weight and/or stretch bands (usually lengths of surgical tubing) to maintain your strength during the ski season. Muscular fitness and flexibility can fade rather quickly, and although maintenance activity won't make you much stronger, it will help you to keep the strength you have worked so hard to develop.

Strength Weights

You will probably find it easiest to use weight rooms for strength workouts and leave all the other weight-oriented workouts (such as circuit or endurance training) for less crowded places. If you have access to a weight room or health club, strength weights can provide useful workouts. If not, then you can incorporate strength work into your program in other ways (see Figure 8.1).

Most skiers can achieve satisfactory results without doing strength weights more than two or three times a week. Remember that many of your other workouts will be more directed toward developing strength. Overdoing strength training can leave you burned out.

Begin doing strength weights rather early in the season. This might seem to contradict our earlier suggestion that you do endurance and base work early in the season. But strength does not come quickly or easily, and if you want to be stronger, you must religiously follow a consistent, long-term strength-training program. Doing strength workouts will not hurt you early in the season as long as you don't burn out and quit too soon. To avoid burnout, set up a strength-training program at the beginning of the summer and plan out the typical workouts you will do in each strength weights session. As the season progresses, keep doing the same exercises but increase repetitions and then increase the weight. Of course, in order to keep increasing your effort throughout the

Figure 8.1 Leg press.

season, you must start off the year at a fairly low level of effort. This type of low-level start to a training year can't hurt you and will keep you from working too hard, too soon.

Typical Strength Weights

We recommend training either the upper body or legs during a single strength weights session and alternating workouts in that fashion. You should do at least some abdominal work in every workout. You are a skier, not a bodybuilder, and your strength-training workouts should emphasize those exercises that use the largest muscle groups. If you have time and energy remaining, go on to the more isolating exercises, but always start the workout with the largest muscle group. For instance, do squats before leg curls and bench presses before tricep curls. We also recommend that you alternate between muscle groups with each exercise. Follow a "pushing" exercise (e.g., bench press) with a "pulling" exercise (e.g., seated rows). The following samples typify this "split" type of workout. If you want to pursue a more complex program, consult the instructor at your local health club or read up on other systems in a source that deals specifically with weight training.

Workout Example: Upper Body.

* BENCH PRESS. 3-5 sets of 8-12 reps with manageable weight.
* SEATED ROWS. 3 sets of 10-15 reps with manageable weight.
* LAT PULLS. 3 sets of 10-15 reps with manageable weight.
* BICEP CURLS. 3 sets of 10-20 reps with manageable weight.
* TRICEP EXTENSIONS. 3 sets of 10-20 reps with manageable weight.
* ABDOMINALS. See the following section on abdominal exercises.

Workout Example: Lower Body.

* SQUATS. 4-6 sets of 10-20 reps with 50-150% of body weight.
* BACK-UPS. 2-3 sets of 15-20 reps with manageable weight.
* LEG PRESS. 3 sets of 10-25 reps with manageable weight.
* LUNGES. 2-3 sets of 20-50 reps with manageable weight.
* LEG CURLS. 3 sets of 8-15 reps with manageable weight.
* LEG EXTENSIONS. 3 sets of 8-15 reps with manageable weight.
* ABDOMINALS. See the following section on abdominal exercises.

Abdominal Exercises (in Every Strength Workout).

Experiment with combinations of sit-ups, abdominal curls, leg lifts, v-sits, and other abdominal exercises. If that gets too easy, use an incline board or hold some weights behind your head. Keep the number of repeti-

Figure 8.2   Abdominal curls.

tions high. Do abdominal exercises near the end of the
workout and do them consistently. Abdominal strength
is vital to maintaining relaxed ski technique (see
Figure 8.2).

Variations.   Change your workouts around occasionally so that your body doesn't get "grooved" to one
particular order or set of exercises. One favorite variation is to devote an entire workout to two or three of
the larger muscle group exercises such as bench press
or squats. Do this by keeping the same weight on the
bar throughout the workout but doing ten sets of
10-15 repetitions, with shorter than normal rests in
between.

Or you can do what are called *increasing sets*. For
increasing sets, do a set number of repetitions for each
exercise and increase the weight each set until you
can no longer do that number of repetitions. When you
reach that point, you can go on to further sets,
decreasing the repetitions while increasing the weight,
until you get down to 4-5 reps.

The key to success with your strength training is
to do it *consistently*. If you are among the many skiers
who don't like strength work very much, the way to
ensure that you do strength workouts consistently is to
make your workouts as interesting and engaging as
possible. Don't be afraid to change your strength workouts around for variety. Keep yourself interested by
setting short-term goals. Remember that you must be
consistent in lifting regularly in order to see positive
results from strength work.

Endurance Weights

Endurance weight training will benefit your progress as a skater more than any other type of weight training. The primary muscles involved in skating are the lower back, gluteals, hamstrings, and quadriceps. The purpose of endurance weight training is to build muscular endurance in these areas. These exercises will be done with relatively light weights, with very high repetitions, at a fairly rapid tempo similar to your stroke tempo on skis (see Figures 8.3-8.7).

Figure 8.3 Bent rows. Keep the knees bent slightly to alleviate strain on the lower back.

Figure 8.4 Squats (endurance weights), to 90 degrees.

Figure 8.5 One-legged squats, to 90 degrees.

Figure 8.6 Step-ups (endurance weights). Begin at 90 degrees, keeping the entire foot on the bench.

Figure 8.7 Back-ups. Keep knees bent slightly. Note how the back is allowed to curl in a relaxed manner, not kept rigid.

Sandbag weights are recommended (but not absolutely necessary) at least for all leg exercises. This is because sandbags are very easy to handle and manage and do not require you to hang onto them at all times during the exercise. Sandbags can be set on the lower back, where the leverage of the exercise will be more efficient in training the muscles involved in skating.

Upper Body

Endurance weight workouts for the upper body always involve exercises that work the largest muscle groups and can be done using sandbags, barbells, pulleys, stretch bands, or body weight for resistance. The emphasis will be on a high number repetitions with moderate weight or resistance. This is where many skiers include poling exercises with an Exer-Genie, roller boards, stretch bands, or dips. Endurance weights can be the most individualized of your workouts. This is an excellent chance to work on your weaknesses, and the workout you design may be longer or shorter than the following example. Don't be

afraid to change any of these workouts around and
tailor them to meet your own needs. They are included
here only to give you some ideas.

Typical Endurance Weights (General, Emphasizing Lower Body).

- SQUATS. 2 sets of 100 reps with 50-150% of body
  weight.
- BENCH PRESS. (or max. push ups) 2 sets of 50
  reps with 15-50% body weight.
- ONE LEG SQUATS. 2 sets of 50 right, 50 left with
  20-50% body weight.
- LAT PULLS. 2 sets of 30-50 reps with 25-75%
  body weight.
- STEP UPS. 50 right, 50 left reps with 20-50% body
  weight.
- BACK-UPS. 50 reps with 15-35% body weight.
- BENT ROWS. 50 reps with 15-25% body weight.
- ABDOMINAL CURLS. 50 reps with 10-25% body
  weight.

Roller Boards.   Long ago skiers discovered the
benefits of using a roller board for building endurance
in the muscles of the arms, back, and shoulders. Roller
boards are one type of equipment in which there is
very little difference between the way skiers have always used the apparatus and the way skating skiers
should use it. We recommend doing an entire workout
on the roller board or fitting it into endurance weights
or circuit workouts. Roller boarding closely simulates
the double-poling motion used in conjunction with
many skating strokes. Because little has changed in
the ways skiers will use the roller board, we will not
discuss it in any more detail. If you do not have a
roller board, a program utilizing stretch bands and
dips can act as a substitute.

When to Begin Endurance Weight Training?
Skiers should probably begin endurance weight workouts in early August and continue them as long as
possible or until a taper toward an important race begins. You may prefer to schedule endurance weight
workouts early in the week (such as on Monday morn-

ing) because these are long and very tiring workouts and might not get done later in the week when you are more fatigued.

Making Sandbag Weights.   Sandbag weights are the easiest thing in the world to make. The ones shown in the illustrations are merely truck tire inner tubes (usually available as discarded seconds from tire stores) that have been cut in half and filled with sand. The ends are twisted and sealed with a few good wrappings of duct tape. Just don't let the neighbors catch you raiding their kids' sandbox! They might not believe your explanation.

A nice set of sandbags is 7, 10, 15, 25, and 35 kilograms. If weights this size seem too cumbersome, you might try adding some lead shot to the sand to make the same weight with less bulk. Some of the larger ones may also be a bit tough to get onto your back. That's another good reason to have a training partner or two around to give you a hand. Sandbags are a very safe way to train. Because of the positioning on your lower back, bending your knees low enough to cause injury is very unlikely. Sandbags also require no spotter to be used safely, even with very heavy weights, because all you need to do to get them off your back is stand up. All of these exercises can be done with a regular set of weights instead of sandbags. Use your imagination a little bit and remember to keep the repetitions high and snappy.

Circuit Training

Earlier we described circuit training as "interval weights," and that is exactly what this workout is. Many skiers like to set up circuit workouts as a series of 10-15 stations that they will run through 1-3 times, with a full rest break between each circuit. Circuit training is a great workout to do with a group of friends because everyone can occupy a station without getting in each other's way and everyone can work at his or her own pace (see Figures 8.8-8.11).

Figure 8.8   V-sits.

Figure 8.9   Discus throw.

Figure 8.10   Back lifts.

Figure 8.11   Squat jumps. Note how the push was made off of the midfoot, not through the toes.

The circuits described here are set up as three circuits of diminishing work periods, such as 12 stations with 60 seconds of work/60 seconds of rest followed by a 5-15 minute rest period, 12 stations with 45 seconds of work/45 seconds rest followed by a full rest, and 12 stations with 30 seconds of work/30 seconds of rest. These can be done in a weight room with conventional weight-lifting equipment if you wish, but you may prefer doing this workout with sandbag weights outdoors on the grass.

In choosing exercises for your circuits, be sure to work every muscle group (especially the legs, hips, and abdominals). Try to space out the exercises in the workout to avoid doing three or four leg stations in a row. Circuit training can be a great workout. Get a group of friends together, crank up the radio, and get loose. This is one of the workouts to enjoy.

Sample Circuit Exercises.

- V-sits
- Push-ups
- Gunther hops with weight
- Roller boarding

- In-and-out jumps with weight
- Abdominal curls with weight
- Squat jumps with weight
- Bent rows
- Forward leg switch with weight
- Discus throw
- Knee-to-chest pulls (right)
- Knee-to-chest pulls (left)
- Back lift

Maintenance Training

Maintenance training won't make you much stronger, but it will prevent all of the strength, flexibility, and muscle endurance that you developed during the dryland season from fading away during the ski season. Skiing itself is not enough to develop or maintain strength or muscle endurance, especially not in the legs. Doing these maintenance exercises on a regular basis in hotel rooms and bus stations will make you a more successful skier. We only hope they don't get you arrested (see Figures 8.12-8.16).

The secret to strength maintenance is to experiment to find your own system and then adhere to the maintenance regimen on a regular basis. Most skiers prefer to begin strength maintenance workouts soon after they get on the snow. We recommend at least two but not more than three times weekly for a single session of maintenance activities. Each session should probably take about an hour and should include both stretch band exercises and body weight exercises such as push-ups, dips, pull-ups, sit-ups, and Wooder squats (which are described in the next section).

Stretch Band Exercises

Many skiers prefer to use a length of surgical tubing called a stretch band as a part of their maintenance training. With this one piece of equipment and a little imagination you can keep almost any part of your body from deteriorating. As shown in Figures 8.12-8.17

Figure 8.12 Wooder squats, to 90 degrees.

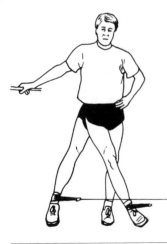

Figure 8.13 Abductions.

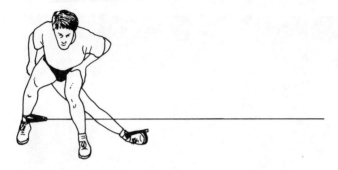

Figure 8.14 Abductions.

Figure 8.15 Adductions.

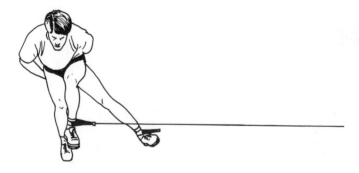

Figure 8.16 Adductions.

Figure 8.17 Knee-to-chest pulls.

stretch band exercises can be used primarily to maintain strength and flexibility in the legs and hips, but there are countless exercises for all body parts that space limitations prevent us from illustrating here. A product called the "Lifeline Gym" has recently come onto the market that is essentially the same as surgical tubing. This device comes equipped with some simple additions that allow you to perform every exercise from squats to bench presses. Although these are a little expensive, they do allow you to perform a lot of good exercises on the road during the ski season or to begin shaping up during the early dryland season.

Wooder Squats

One of the legendary figures in recent American speed skating is Dr. Mike Woods. Dr. Woods, known to his friends as "Wooder," is a practicing anesthesiologist in a Milwaukee hospital who managed to work his way through medical school and practice medicine while earning positions on three Olympic teams. To do this, he obviously had to be very motivated and highly imaginative in squeezing workouts into a very busy schedule. The invention of his that allowed him to do this and that will most benefit you as a skating skier is an exercise called, appropriately, *Wooder squats.*

Wooder squats are a simple exercise that can serve as a part of a maintenance workout or as an entire workout when you don't have the time for anything

longer. The Wooder squat is a one-legged squat (down
to a 90-degree knee bend) that is performed for a predetermined time and followed by a shorter rest period
before switching to squats on the other leg. This cycle
can continue (in series of 40 seconds of work/20 seconds of rest) from 5 to 30 minutes.

Wooder squats will make you sore, so don't do
them the night before a big race. They can also pose
potential problems for people with bad knees. Give
them a try if you want, but use some restraint if
you're worried. As with all other skating exercises,
start out with short sessions and build up gradually.
Ease off if your knees give you any trouble.

All of these exercises will help you to maintain
your level of dryland fitness during the ski season. You
should follow whatever system is most manageable for
you that you can keep up consistently.

Schedule Planning

9

The purpose of this book is to help you to direct yourself as a skating skier and learn how to arrange your training schedules. This chapter will deal with the basic elements of setting up a training program. This information will enable you to plan and develop your own training schedule to suit your own needs, goals, and abilities. The ideas presented in this chapter are not reviews of what skiers have done to train for skating in the past. The systems devised in the past, especially by American skiers, have proven inadequate in training skating skiers. This chapter includes new ideas that reflect a future direction in how skiers should train for best performance in skating races.

The skiing training season actually covers the entire year beginning with 3 to 10 weeks of rest and recreation immediately following the competitive ski season. This training year can be broken down by month, week, and day, and basic elements should be applied to each of these training periods.

Year Planning

The training year is the easiest period to plan but the hardest schedule to live up to. It is easiest to think of the training year as divided into six phases of training emphasis.

Phase 1 (8-12 Weeks) May to July

At the beginning of the training season the goal for all skiers should be to begin building an *endurance*

base. The best way to do this is through primarily
nontechnical, nonspecific workouts such as biking,
running, and rowing. Many skiers feel the urge to begin the dryland season on roller skis or roller skates.
This is a serious error that will cause technical problems later in the season and could lead to injury in
joints and muscles that have not yet been adequately
conditioned to take on the stresses of the skating
stroke. Skating technique is too strenuous to be performed properly for any length of time without first
developing a sound training base. Roller skiing in May
will lead either to bad technical habits from doing
workouts without the strength to maintain proper
technique or to injury from striving to maintain proper
technique when the body is not yet prepared to do so.
Be patient at this time of year. Condition your muscles
and develop your overall fitness before you try to con-
quer technique. Concentrate on becoming a good skier
only after your body is prepared to do so. Most of the
workouts in this period should concentrate on endurance. Very little tempo or heavy weight work should
be done in this period.

Phase 2 (8-12 Weeks) July to October

This is when skiers should begin to concentrate on
ski-specific dryland workouts. Having achieved a
proper fitness base in Phase 1, you can now move on
to the more technical elements of summer training.
We advise beginning this more specific phase of training with the inclusion of simulation exercises to build
up the skating muscles. This will soon be followed by
the inclusion of slideboarding, roller skiing, and roller
skating. Keep up your nontechnical workouts because
much of your roller skiing and roller skating will be
done in technique-only workouts. To keep up this
schedule many skiers find that they need to train
twice a day. You will do some of your most intense
training during Phase 2 and continue this intensity until you get on the snow. Many skiers also begin more
intense strength training, tempos, and interval workouts at this time. You should increase your total train-

ing time, individual workout intensity, and the specificity of workouts during this period.

Phase 3 (3-6 Weeks) Mid-October to November

The transition from dryland training to on-snow training is tough for many skiers. This is when you discover just how much all that summer training is going to improve your ski season performance. Use this time to practice correct ski technique on the snow while devoting the bulk of your strenuous workouts to dryland activities. Try to do most of your skiing on the flats to practice all strokes and transitions. Use technical intervals for a large part of your skiing workouts. Don't make the mistake of discontinuing your dryland work as soon as the first snow falls. The ski season is long, and the beginning is no time to neglect the technical elements that will be so vital later in the season.

Phase 4 (10-15 Weeks) November to Late December

We call this phase *on-snow training.* The transition from dryland to snow and most of the dryland exercises are behind you now. During Phase 4 the majority of your training is done on the snow. By now your skiing technique should be fairly solid, and you are free to concentrate on high-quality skiing workouts. Add practice races and more intense workouts such as sprints, hill work, intervals, and tempos to your training schedule. Strength maintenance workouts should begin at this time, and strength weights and endurance weights should be reduced.

Phase 5 (2-4 Weeks) January or February to March

These weeks will be spent in the *long taper,* which will be described in the next section of this chapter. Your success in planning this crucial period will determine how well you perform in your most important event. After the season's primary taper the rest of your time will be spent in racing and recreational skiing.

Phase 6 (4-8 Weeks) April to May

Phase 6 is a rest period at the end of the skiing year. Use this time to get away from skiing for a while to clear your mind and allow yourself a chance to relax. Depending on where you live, this phase will usually last until the end of April.

Guidelines for Planning the Training Year

1. You must begin the year slowly, even though this is probably the time when you are most enthusiastic about training (see Figure 9.1). The yearly schedule should begin with low intensity, nontechnical workouts. You will do yourself no good by starting roller ski training in May.
2. As the dryland season progresses, your workouts should become more intense and more specific. Develop your fitness base in nontechnical workouts.

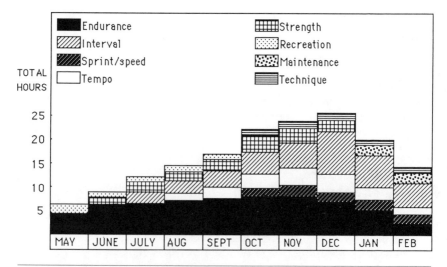

Figure 9.1 This graph illustrates the general increase in intensity and specificity of workouts in planning the training year.

3. When making the transition from dryland to on-snow training, devote the first week or two to technical skiing workouts, primarily on the flat. During this time, most of your hard workouts should still be dryland workouts. Don't sacrifice your technique on the first day of snow by trying to go out too hard, too soon.

4. Maintain a certain amount of dryland work throughout the ski season, especially strength maintenance work. Skiing itself is not enough to keep you in optimal shape for skiing.

5. Build your effort toward optimal performance in specific, preplanned competitions. If you expect to be at your best every race and every weekend, then you'll get nothing but disappointing results. We will explore this strategy in greater depth in our discussion of "tapering."

6. Take a full break when the season is over. Starting the new training season the day after the last one is completed is sure to leave you burned out and tired of training by midsummer.

We will try to illustrate all these principles in the next chapter by showing you a typical training program.

Tapering

In the course of your training regimen, occasionally you will have a day when no one can keep up with you and you feel like you can beat the world. On days like these, you think to yourself, "If only I could feel like this when it counts!" One of the major differences between the most successful skiers and the perpetual runners up is that successful skiers arrange their workout schedules and regulate their level of effort in such a way that they will be more likely to feel and perform their best on the day of the race. Understanding the principles of "tapering" allows them to do this.

Sometimes called *peaking*, tapering is the gradual process of decreasing the quantity of your training work load so that when the day of competition arrives you will be completely rested but not to the point where you have begun to decondition. This is more difficult than it sounds. The purpose of this section is to outline a system for the skating skier to taper properly.

What's New About Tapering?

Since the advent of skating techniques, the practice of tapering has changed for cross-country skiers. Tapering can no longer be thought of as simply that time at which an athlete's oxygen uptake is at its highest point. Skiing has become more like rowing and speed skating in that effective tapering for skiing now involves a muscular consideration. Regardless of their oxygen uptake, skiers cannot perform optimally if skating muscles are not completely recovered from training. Tapering for skiers now involves more complete muscular rest before the targeted competition, as you will see in the very low work loads in the following examples. This means that skating skiers will be resting more completely, especially in the last week before a competition, than they might have when using conventional cross-country techniques, which are less taxing to the major muscles. Because endurance fades sooner than strength, skiers must find ways to continue training for endurance during a taper period without overworking the skating muscles. The easiest solution to this problem is to do your endurance skiing during the taper in the form of intervals (rather than long endurance skiing) and to keep some foot running (or some other aerobic activity) in your training program.

Why Is Tapering So Difficult?

Tapering poses three tough problems.

1. To taper effectively, you must know yourself very well, both as a person and as an athlete. You must be honest with yourself in assessing your potential for the particular competition you have targeted and taper accordingly. This means working hard

right up until the taper begins, even though you may be getting disappointing race results. Skiers must trust the workout schedule to bring them to a level of peak performance at the targeted time.

2. You may be participating in a dozen or more races during the winter season. If you try to peak for all of them, you will spend all your time resting instead of training. The key is to convince yourself that most of your races are for practice and experience and be able to swallow your pride now and then in order to maximize your performance for selected competitions. The fewer times you attempt to peak for certain events, the more effective your tapering will be.

3. If, like many skiers, you come to enjoy your training and the way it makes you feel on a day-to-day basis, then tapering at the time of the season when skiing and performance are most important may make you irritable and nervous. More than one skier has finally broken down and gone out for a long endurance ski or a tough tempo workout the day before a big race. It's understandable to feel this way. The nervousness of a big competition will make you uneasy, and proving to yourself that you can still do a good, hard workout would boost your confidence before the big event. In a situation like this, all we can suggest is to relax and try to draw your confidence from all the training you have done in the past months. Remember that going out and pushing yourself before a key race can only hurt your performance.

Long or Short Taper?

It would be no fun if you had spent a whole year in training for just one competition and had to waste all those other weekends on bad performances. Remember that tapering too much is like not training at all. The way to compromise in this situation is to develop two types of tapers: a long one for the most important competition and a short one for the qualifiers or slightly less important competitions where a good performance is still needed.

Short Taper. Use a short taper to rest up a bit for a less important competition. If the race is on Saturday, begin resting on the preceding Tuesday or Wednesday. And we mean *resting*. This is similar to what is called a *drop taper*, meaning that your work load will continue at a high level up until 3-5 days before the targeted event. The last few days will be spent in short speed work and easy intervals. During this period you should not do any long-distance workouts or tempos. Just spend those days allowing your system to clean itself out. This type of taper is intended to allow your muscles to rid themselves of stiffness and waste products in time for the targeted event. Because of the short duration of the drop taper, your endurance base will not suffer as long as you do not try this too many times during the season. Immediately following the race, you should return to a heavy work load as though nothing had happened.

This is not something to try every weekend. Don't use this short taper more than two or three times during the ski season. The fewer times you need to taper, the more effective each one will be. The key is to get over the insecurity that makes you want to avoid training through a race. When training through a race your work load will remain high right up to the night before the race. The race itself will just count as a hard workout and good experience. This can be awful for your morale, but only if you allow it to be. Keep in mind that your training and performance are designed to keep you improving *throughout* the ski season. If winning the first race of the year becomes too important, your performance may never improve for the remainder of the season. Pick your important events and shoot for good performances at those. Devote the rest of the racing year to acquiring experience.

Long Taper. Use a long taper to prepare for that one event that is more important to you than all the others. The term *taper* is derived from the type of gradual, drawn-out decrease in quality and quantity of work load typical of the long taper. The younger the athlete is, the shorter the taper can be. For most people a long taper can be anywhere from 2-3 weeks in length.

A long taper is nothing like a short taper. The level of the work load in a long taper should never decrease to the minimal level of a short taper. At the beginning of a long taper, the decrease in work load will be so minimal that it is practically invisible. The total decrease in the work load of a long taper should be very gradual, beginning with a reduction in weights, maintenance work, tempos, and strength work. The basic formula is to decrease effort in all these areas 20-30 percent every week, and then cease them completely 5-7 days before the targeted competition.

The length and intensity of endurance workouts will also gradually decrease in the 3-week cycle, but not to such an extreme degree. Avoid long-distance ski workouts in the last 4-6 days before the targeted competition. This may sound odd to some of you who are accustomed to conventional skiing, so it needs to be explained. The problem with skating in general is that it is very inefficient at low speeds (such as in an long, easy, recreational ski). Skating will end up tiring your leg muscles almost as much at low speeds as at high speeds because at a low, relaxed stroke tempo you will be forcing each leg into longer periods of static muscle activity. It may not feel so bad during that easy ski the night before the race, but on race day your legs will have no snap. If you are afraid of losing endurance during tapering, try running easily, stationary bicycling, walking on a treadmill, or even some conventional skiing. But be careful that those "easy ski" workouts don't spoil your race!

The workouts that will change the least during a long taper are the intervals, which will continue at an almost normal rate up until 3-4 days before the competition, and sprints, which will be held at a normal level until 6-7 days before the competition and then dropped completely. It is through intervals that you will be able to maintain your endurance without losing your snap. Intervals raise your heart rate enough to provide perfectly adequate endurance workouts while keeping the work loads low enough to allow your muscles to recover.

Guidelines for Tapering.

1. The younger the athlete, the shorter the taper should be. Athletes under the age of 15 need almost no taper other than a full day of rest to perform at full capacity, whereas athletes over 30 may require a full month.

2. For best results, taper as seldom as possible. Limit yourself to one long taper per season, and no more than 2-3 short tapers per season.

3. A short taper is a short-term, extreme drop in work load, usually beginning 3-5 days before the targeted event.

4. A long taper is a long, gradual decrease in the work load, generally as long as 2-3 weeks.

5. A long taper begins with reductions in work load quantity (20-30% per week) over the first half of the taper period. This is followed in the second half of the taper by continued quantity reductions up until the targeted event.

6. In the last few days before the targeted event, the rule of tapering is "If you feel good, stop and go home." The reason for this attitude is that if you have been training and tapering properly, you will start feeling great, physically and technically. Many people forget that this surge is the result of the resting they have been doing. They want to go out and ski even harder while they are feeling so good. Don't forget what you have been resting for. If you push yourself when your body is beginning to taper, you could end up flat on competition day.

Remember that this is all our personal system and that it may not work as well for you as it has for us. For this reason we are not going to show you an actual copy of our taper programs. What we suggest is not what you want to hear: Experiment with your tapering and keep a record of your results. That is the only way to find out what is best for *you*. We have included these tapering guidelines only to give you some initial direction.

You can get some idea of the type of work reduction we are talking about by going over the programs in chapter 10.

Overtraining. In every athlete's training program there is the risk of going overboard and working too hard. To maintain an effective training program, you must press yourself close to the edge of your work capacity. It is not at all easy to maintain this level of intensity of performance without going too far every once in a while.

If you find yourself on the verge of overtraining, the only thing to do is back off for a while until your body can recover. Watch for the warning signs that your body will give you. An increase in your normal resting pulse rate, insomnia or need for more than normal sleep, weight loss, moodiness and bad attitude may mean that you have been training too hard. Taking it a little easier is all that will bring you back. Sheer physical burnout like this cannot be trained through.

Month Planning

Break up months by varying weekly intensity. The following description is a very common, 4-week system: 3 weeks of increasing intensity followed by a week of lower intensity to allow the body to recover; Week 1 moderate, Week 2 more intense, Week 3 hard, followed by Week 4, an "easy week." The other planning system that is very popular among skiers is a hard day/easy day system. In this system a hard day is followed by a less intense day or a day of rest to allow your body enough time to recover. There are many other systems like these all lumped under the heading of "periodization." For the sake of convenience I have chosen to cover only the 4-week periodization system.

4-Week Guidelines

1. Don't let an easy week get too easy. Drop weight training from this week's program and lower the intensity of all other workouts, but don't get too lazy.

2. Week 3 (hard week) should be very intense. To prepare for this, try your best to get other distractions out of the way before this week begins. It's not a good idea to plan a hard week during final exams, job interviews, or apartment hunting. Try to plan something nice for the end of the week to give yourself something to look forward to.

3. Make up your workout plans at the beginning of each month and try your best to keep up with the schedule you have set. This means that you will have to be realistic in your planning.

4. Set short-term goals so that you can see some progress in your training. If the only goals you have cannot be realized until next winter, you may become depressed by your apparent lack of progress. Keeping yourself in a positive frame of mind is one of the most important elements of your training.

Week Planning

All the planning described in this chapter can be attributed to common sense. The only reason we include it here is that generating this common sense took us about 6 years of mistakes and ignorance, and we want to spare you that grief and frustration. Many outstanding athletes are constantly reminding themselves of all these things, so don't be insulted if some of our suggestions seem a little obvious.

1. Plan to do the workouts you dislike the most early in the week so that at the end of the week, when you are worn out, you will be more likely to do the workouts you enjoy the most.

2. Try not to neglect your weaknesses. Address your weaknesses by scheduling those toughest workouts at the easiest possible time on the most convenient day.

3. Plan to do easy or short workouts (such as sprint work) at the least convenient times. This workout is easy, short, and enjoyable enough that you can probably get through it at a less convenient time.

4. Keep whichever training rituals yield good results in your training program. For example, maybe you plan to keep hill tempos on Sunday mornings, forever. If you are very comfortable with a certain part of your schedule and look forward to it every week, why change it?
5. Set weekly goals for your number of training hours. Keep track of those hours so that you can regulate your intensity through the training year.

Weekly Training Hours

For years skiers have kept track of their weekly training programs by totalling their number of training hours. This can still be practiced in a skating program but some special considerations need to be made in recording your training hours. Training for skating skiers will generally be more intense and of shorter duration than for traditional ski training. We recommend adding strength-training hours and all other workouts to achieve a weekly total. Don't forget to include all time spent warming up, warming down, and resting in between sets. A very intense workout may include only 20-30 minutes of actual work time, but total time, including between sets, may add up to 90 minutes or more.

Programs will vary according to personal preferences and individual needs. Weekly hours for an elite skier may range from as few as 5-6 hours per week in May to as many as 20-25 hours per week in December. You will need to decide for yourself how much time you can devote to your skiing program and how much capacity for work you possess.

On the next page is a brief rundown of average training hours during Week 3 of these monthly programs for an elite skier.

Day Planning

The only times that daily planning becomes an important decision is when you are sick, injured, or overtrained or when you plan to do more than one

Month	Hours per week	Program additions/instructions
May	5-8	Begin easy training.
June	7-10	Emphasize endurance training. Begin strength weights.
July	9-12	Introduce intervals, specific exercises, and roller skiing.
Aug.	10-14	Introduce tempos and endurance weights.
Sept.	12-16	Lengthen tempos and increase intervals.
Oct.	15-19	Introduce sprint work and technical-only workouts.
Nov.	18-22	Finally on snow. Drop dryland technical work. Continue nontechnical dryland workouts.
Dec.	20-25	Reduce endurance work on snow. Reduce all weight training 20%. Emphasize intervals and tempos. Begin strength maintenance work.
Jan.	12-16 (taper)	Further reduce low-quality endurance work. Reduce weight training another 30%. Begin long taper.
Feb.	10-14	Drop weight training entirely. Decrease quantity of all work. Concentrate on race performance.
March	8-12	Concentrate on racing, short tempos, and intervals.
April	8 or less	Concentrate on racing and spring skiing. Don't worry about workouts at all. Go out when you feel like it and enjoy the weather!

workout that day. If you are sick or injured, let common sense be your guide and don't be afraid to take a day off.

As for double workout days, here are a few guidelines to follow, as well as some general daily guidelines that should be followed in planning any training day.

1. Try not to work the same system or major muscle group twice in the same day. In other words, don't do weights twice, two endurance workouts, or two tempo workouts in a single day. Mix it up a little. This will provide your body sufficient time to recover and gain full benefit from the workouts.
2. If you have planned a technical workout for a certain day, try to do that one first. Otherwise you may be so tired from your nontechnical workout that it will affect your technical ability.
3. Be sure to get enough rest every day, especially on double workout days. You can't make up your rest on another day.
4. If you are especially tired or in a very wrong frame of mind, don't be afraid to skip a workout entirely

or at least change it to something you can toler-
ate. If you do skip a day, don't try to make it up
and don't feel guilty about it. If you get too con-
cerned about the workouts you have missed, you
may end up too neurotic to get out and do the rest
of them on your schedule.

5. Schedule your workouts at a time of day when the
   conditions will be bearable. Make it easy for yourself. If you schedule all your August workouts at
   noon to make yourself tougher, you will probably
   end up skipping more workouts than you otherwise might. We realize that you will need to work
   around school or employment schedules, so be
   reasonable in how you plan your days. Always
   remember that rest can be just as important as
   working out.

6. Realize that you will not always be able to schedule your workouts at convenient, comfortable
   times. These are the times when you will need to
   motivate yourself into going out and getting it
   done. This is when your goals are important. If
   you have set goals that you can achieve in training, these will help to motivate you on those down
   days. Try to set short-term goals on a daily,
   weekly, and monthly basis as well as long-term,
   larger skiing goals to maximize your motivation
   and realize your progress.

Sample Programs

10

This is a high-level ski training program, illustrated as the third weeks (hard weeks) from selected months of a typical year. It is designed for a very advanced skier with a complete training base. It is not intended that you follow this program to the letter. Hopefully, by looking it over, you will see some helpful patterns and get some good workout ideas. I have left out any mention of warm-up or warm-down in these workout descriptions. We are assuming that all skiers warm up and warm down thoroughly for each workout.

June. Third week's workouts; approximately 10 hours (see Figure 10.1).

	Mon.	Tues.	Wed.	Thurs.	Fri.	Sat.	Sun.
AM	Dynamic endurance cycle	Endurance run		Rest	Strength weights	Dynamic run	
PM	Strength weights		Endurance cycle	Rest			Endurance cycle or recreation

Figure 10.1 June, Week 3.

Dynamic endurance cycle. 1-2 hours over flat or rolling terrain with 6 speed increases of 3 minutes.
Strength weights. Personal preference.
Endurance run. Steady state run of 45-90 minutes.
Endurance cycle. Steady state ride over flattest terrain; all spinning; 1-3 hours.
Dynamic run. 45-minute run. Take good warm-up, run hard 1 minute out of every 5 minutes.
Strength weights. Personal preference.
Endurance cycle. Long, easy ride over rolling terrain. Work the hills.

August. Third week's workouts; approximately 15 hours (see Figure 10.2).

	Mon.	Tues.	Wed.	Thurs.	Fri.	Sat.	Sun.
AM	Endurance weights	Endurance run dry skate	Interval tour	Rest	Dynamic roller ski	Circuit	Endurance slideboard
PM	Roller ski natural intervals	Strength weights	Tempo runs	Rest	Bike intervals		Endurance cycle or recreation

Figure 10.2   August, Week 3.

Endurance weights. 1 x all exercises.
    Squats. 100 reps with manageable weight.
    Bent rows. 50 reps with manageable weight.
    One-legged squats. 50 right and 50 left with manageable weight.
    Back-ups. 50 reps with manageable weight.
    Step-ups. 50 right and 50 left with manageable weight.
    Abdominal curls. 50 reps with manageable weight.
Roller skiing, natural intervals. 1 hour or more in hilly terrain. Go hard on all uphills, moderate on flats; coast all downhills.

Endurance run/dry skate. 3-minute jog rest between each set.

> 5 minutes: different exercise every minute.
> 3 minutes: dry skating.
> 2 minutes: Gunther hops.
> 1 minute: squat jumps.
> 2 minutes: forward leg switch.
> 3 minutes: dry skating.
> 5 minutes: switching exercises on the minute.

Strength weights. Personal preference.

Interval tour. 60 minutes.

Tempo runs. 5-, 4-, 3-, 2.5-, 2-, 1.5-, 1-, .5-minute tempo runs; full rest between each.

Dynamic roller ski. 2-hour moderate ski; increase pace for 2 minutes in every 10-minute section.

Bike intervals. 3 sets of 10 reps of 20 seconds on/40 seconds off.

Circuit. See circuit training instructions in chapter 5.

Endurance slideboard. 2 sets consisting of 2-minute warm-up, 3 reps of 10-minute slideboarding concentrating on low body position and exaggerating technique, followed by 2-minute easy warm-down.

Endurance cycle. 2-hour or more steady state ride. Spin as much as possible.

October. Third week's workouts; approximately 20 hours (see Figure 10.3).

	Mon.	Tues.	Wed.	Thurs.	Fri.	Sat.	Sun.
AM	Endurance weights	Interval slideboard	Roller ski short intervals	Rest	Roller skate technique	Circuit	Hill tempos
PM	Roller ski long intervals	Strength weights	Bike tempos	Rest	Sprint runs	Dynamic roller ski	Endurance cycle or recreation

Figure 10.3 October, Week 3.

Endurance weights. 2 reps of all exercises.
Roller skiing, long intervals. 10 reps of 5 minutes on/2.5 minutes off.
Interval slideboard. 5-minute warm-up, 12 reps of 2.5 minutes on/1.5 minutes off, 5-minute warm-down.
Strength weights. Personal preference.
Roller skiing, short interval. 2 sets of 10 reps of 60 seconds on/60 seconds off. Rest 4-10 minutes between each set.
Bike tempos. 5-, 3-, 2-, 1-, 2-, 3-, 5-minute tempos; full rest between each one.
Roller skating technique. 10 reps of 2 minutes on/ 1 minute off; low effort.
Sprint runs. See instructions in chapter 5.
Circuit. See instructions in chapter 5.
Dynamic roller skiing. 1-2 hour ski over rollng terrain. Increase effort for 3 minutes of every 12-minute section.
Hill tempos. 10 reps of 1-5 minutes uphill tempo run and low walk.
Endurance cycle. 1-3 hour steady state ride over rolling terrain.

Depending on where you live, you should be able to get on the snow some time in October or November. During this time of transition from dryland to on-snow training, you should make a point to continue your nontechnical dryland workouts. Use your skiing time to sharpen technical skills with low effort drills on the flats. After the first week or two you will be able to begin doing hard workouts on the snow.

December. Third week's workouts; approximately 24 hours, including racing (see Figure 10.4).
Long tempos. 4 reps of 5 kilometers; long rests between each. Warm down thoroughly.
Technique only. 30 reps of 100 meters; very low level of effort. Concentrate on proper technique. Mix up stroke styles and practice transitions.
Endurance weights. 2 x all exercises.
Dynamic endurance. 20 kilometers at moderate pace with 1 kilometer at increased effort every 3 kilometers.
Short tempos. 20 reps of .5 kilometers. Use same loop each set and keep track of times. Stop if time ever gets markedly slower.

	Mon.	Tues.	Wed.	Thurs.	Fri.	Sat.	Sun.
AM	Long tempos	Dynamic endurance	Short tempos (speed)	Long intervals	Dynamic endurance run	Race	Race
PM	Technique only	Endurance weights	Strength weights	Endurance (natural interval)	Short intervals		Endurance (natural interval)

Figure 10.4 December, Week 3.

Strength weights. Reduced.
Long intervals. 10 sets of 5 minutes on/2 minutes off.
Natural intervals. 90-minute natural interval. Work uphills, coast downhills.
Endurance run. 30-45 minutes steady state.
Short intervals. 3 sets of 10 reps of 40 seconds on/20 seconds off.
Natural intervals. 60-minute natural interval.

February. Third week's workouts; approximately 15 hours, including racing (see Figure 10.5).
Long tempos. 5 sets of 3 kilometers; long rests.
Technique only. 20 sets of 100 meters. Concentrate on technique only.
Long intervals. 20 kilometers. Ski 4 kilometers at increased effort, followed by 1 kilometer at very low effort.
Short tempos. 20 sets of 200 meters. First 10 on the flat, second 10 uphill; very intense effort and full rests between each set. Be careful not to get too cold between sets. Keep track of time for each 200 meters. Stop when you become markedly slower.
Strength maintenance. 1 rep of all stretch band exercises and 1 rep of all favorite upper-body and abdominal exercises. Don't overdo it.
Short intervals. 5 kilometers of 45 seconds on/45 seconds off. Or set up an Indian line: Person at the rear

	Mon.	Tues.	Wed.	Thurs.	Fri.	Sat.	Sun.
AM	Long tempos	Long intervals	Short tempos	Rest	Short intervals	Race	Race
PM	Technique only		Strength maint.				Endurance (natural intervals)

Figure 10.5   February, Week 3.

passes all and moves to the front. Keep line short
enough that you will do enough intervals over
5 kilometers.
Natural intervals. 60-minute interval tour. Do this
very soon after the day's racing.

Equipment for Skating

11

In keeping with the nature of the rest of this book, the only reason a chapter on equipment exists is that a number of technological developments have occurred, which make equipment selection something new for many skiers. Many products have come onto the market specifically for the skating skier. These include almost every part of skiing equipment, from skis and poles to bindings and boots.

The primary technological development has been to stiffen everything in sight. Skis have become shorter, poles have become longer, and shoes and bindings have become more torsionally rigid. All these pieces of equipment have become stiffer in response to the extra stresses put on them by the skating skier. Skating can be done very well without specialized equipment, but if you can afford it, why not make it as easy as possible? The specialized equipment that will be described here is beneficial but not absolutely necessary for the skating skier. Choose your equipment based on your own needs and hope for a few special sales along the way. This chapter presents some suggestions and guidelines for selecting equipment.

Poles

The trend among skating skiers has been to select longer poles. This is primarily the result of the increased speed available to the skater. Your poling is mainly involved in speed maintenance. Average speed with skating techniques is considerably higher than in conventional skiing, and using a longer set of poles helps to supply more leverage at this high speed. At these speeds, many skiers also feel that shorter poles throw off their balance.

All the better racing poles you'll be seeing in the local ski shop this winter will be extra-stiff, carbon- or boron-reinforced shafts, hopefully available in proper long lengths. In the past couple of years, there has been a shortage of long poles. Even though they are prohibitively expensive, try racing and training with a quality pair of poles. Keep a few different lengths in your closet for different conditions. The slower or hillier the course, the shorter your poles should be. Also remember that longer, inflexible poles tend to break easily, especially in crowded packs or acrobatic falls.

What Length?

Although personal preference is still the best guide for pole length, people have been searching for guidelines to assist first-time buyers. The most useful general guideline is that most skiers seem to be most efficient using poles that reach the upper lip (measured in street shoes). That measure usually accounts for approximately 90 percent of your height (a 5'10" skier might use 162.5-cm poles). In choosing your particular pole length, keep the following three guidelines in mind:

1. If you are just beginning to experiment with a longer pole in your skiing, try to increase your pole lengths in reasonable intervals. Don't jump from 145 centimeters. Get used to your longer poles on roller skis or roller skates before the actual ski season begins.
2. Many skiers choose poles that are much too long. Don't get caught up in the frenzy over long poles. There is a point where your poles are so long that you can no longer plant them accurately or maintain the proper tempo. You can always find a use for poles that are slightly too short, but a pair that is too long will only gather dust in the closet until your giant friends come to visit.

3. The new skiing rules dictate that your poles cannot be taller than you are. Don't laugh; skiers were heading in that direction before the rules stopped them.

Skis

Whereas poles have become longer, skis have become shorter. As with the trend toward longer poles, the degree to which skis can be shortened has been halted by new rules and common sense. Skiers began using shorter skis for two reasons: Shorter skis are stiffer and can transfer force more efficiently into the snow, and they are also easier to handle in maintaining a high stroke tempo. Many skiers felt clumsy performing skating movements on the longer skis.

At least among accomplished skiers, this trend toward shorter skis has leveled off. Skiers are remembering that skiing is a gliding sport and that longer skis glide faster. With practice, you can learn to control a ski that is slightly longer than what many skiers use for skating and thus gain the advantages of increased glide. Once again the issue becomes a question of what is most comfortable for the individual. The ski that you will ski fastest on is whatever ski is the longest one that you can control without hampering your skating stroke.

Ski Shopping

When shopping for racing skis, there are a few key considerations for the skating skier. You are looking for a stiffer ski, or what manufacturers designate as a *skating ski*. The variables to consider deal mainly with the ski bottoms. Many new models have three grooves in the bottom of the ski (as opposed to one in more conventional skis). This allows the ski to track much better in the absence of tracks (which today means most of the time). Early reactions to these three-grooved skis have been very positive.

Also consider the following factors when choosing a skating ski:

1. There are two new rules pertaining to ski specifications: Both skis must be the same length and cannot be shorter than the skier, and no *exposed* metal edges are allowed on the bottoms.
2. Some new models have a short, stylized ski tip called a *nose*. This feature is designed to allow more ski mobility and lessen the chance of catching a tip in soft snow. Many skiers have been cutting off the tips of their old skis to lighten the fronts, thus making it easy to keep the tips from dragging. This is recommended if the skis you choose don't feel weighted correctly. Just be sure that you seal the exposed end with epoxy to keep water from seeping in.
3. The markings on a conventional ski that direct you where to mount the bindings are a little too far forward for easiest skating. Many skiers are more comfortable if the bindings are set 1.5 centimeters farther back than the markings suggest. You should consult with the person who is mounting your skis; that person should know most about the product and the manufacturer's recommendations. If you end up moving a set of bindings, be sure to adequately seal up the old holes.

Boots and Bindings

For most people, the boots and bindings they have been using will be more than adequate for skating purposes. The better your skating technique, the less you need the torsional rigidity and extra stiffness of the new skating equipment. On the other hand, why not take every advantage that your pocketbook can afford? The extra stiffness in these new products will help you to keep your technique when your physiological tools are failing you. All the boot companies are coming out with skating equipment this season, so you might as well give them a look.

A Final Word

This book has tried to give skiers some direction in pursuing the techniques of skating on cross-country skis. The ideas expressed here and the skating techniques themselves are so new that much more information will undoubtedly emerge in the next few years. Our goal has been to provide you with some guidelines for interpreting other innovations that are bound to occur. The information we have presented will give you some feeling for the future direction of cross-country skiing. If this book succeeds in reaching a fairly large audience, then at least skiers will be able to discuss and argue with a greater understanding of the sport.

If you have found some of our ideas to be controversial and provocative, then our goal has been achieved. A book like this can only reflect one set of opinions accurately. A little lively argument can only enrich the body of technical knowledge in the skiing world. We hope that the information we have compiled will help to get you started as a skating skier. If this book succeeds in doing that, then our effort was worthwhile.

Index